WHISTLEBLOWING RESEARCH

Methodological and Moral Issues

by
Frederick Elliston
John Keenan
Paula Lockhart
and Jane van Schaick

PRAEGER

PRAEGER SPECIAL STUDIES • PRAEGER SCIENTIFIC

New York • Philadelphia • Eastbourne, UK
Toronto • Hong Kong • Tokyo • Sydney

Library of Congress Cataloging in Publication Data

Main entry under title:

Whistleblowing research.

   Includes index.
   1. Whistle blowing—United States. I. Elliston,
Frederick.
HD60.5.U5W4735   1984   331'.01   84-13293
ISBN 0-03-070777-3 (alk. paper)

Published in 1985 by Praeger Publishers
CBS Educational and Professional Publishing
a Division of CBS Inc.
521 Fifth Avenue, New York, NY 10175 USA

ACKNOWLEDGMENTS

Our work was conducted under a grant (NSF OSS-8006553) from a program on Ethical Values in Science and Technology (EVIST), jointly sponsored by the National Endowment for the Humanities (NEH) and the National Science Foundation (NSF).

We would like to thank the members of the Michael J. Hindelang Research Center at the State University of New York, Albany, for their patience and advice and the staff of the Center for the Study of Ethics in the Professions at the Illinois Institute of Technology for their support and suggestions.

CONTENTS

LIST OF ABBREVIATIONS

BART	Bay Area Rapid Transit
EPA	Environmental Protection Agency
FBI	Federal Bureau of Investigation
FLRA	Federal Labor Relations Authority
GAO	General Accounting Office
GAP	Government Accountability Project
GSA	General Services Administration
HEW	Health, Education and Welfare
IPS	Institute for Policy Studies
MSPB	Merit Systems Protection Board
NFSO	Navy Fuel Supply Office
NLRA	National Labor Relations Board
NORC	National Opinion Research Center
OPM	Office of Personnel Management
OSC	Office of Special Counsel

PART ONE
CONCEPTS, THEORIES AND METHOD

ONE
A CONCEPTUAL
ANALYSIS

INTRODUCTION

In recent years we have been reading more and more about a phenomenon that is metaphorically called "blowing the whistle." This is due, at least in part, to several widely publicized incidents of whistleblowing [1] and legislative activities aimed at protecting government whistleblowers.[2] This has happened at a time when there is growing interest in business and professional ethics, and, as a result, philosophers and sociologists have begun to discuss the ethical and sociological issues posed by whistleblowing.[3] For ethicists the most important issue is when, if ever, it is morally permissible or obligatory for an individual to blow the whistle. The issue is difficult because blowing the whistle may cause harm to the whistleblower and those accused, while not blowing the whistle may cause harm to those who are the victims of the unreported wrongdoing. For those interested in organizational structures and the protection of the public good, whistleblowing brings to the fore questions about management policies and organizational mechanisms designed to encourage socially responsible behavior. Whatever the concern, whistleblowing raises fundamental questions about the duties of employees to their employers and the duties of employers to their employees.

The purpose of this chapter is not, however, to tackle any of these difficult questions, but to clear the way for them by answering a prior question: what is whistleblowing?

We cannot know whether an act is morally required or morally permissible until we know the character of the act. We cannot discuss strategies for eliminating the need to blow the whistle until we know what it is that is achieved by blowing the whistle. Yet authors of the major works on whistleblowing have paid little attention to definition.[4]

SEVERAL DEFINITIONS

The phrase "blowing the whistle" and the label "whistleblower" have entered our language as metaphors and consequently have been used very loosely.[5] A definition of whistleblowing is needed that captures the essential features of ordinary usage and yet has the precision that is necessary for philosophical, legal, or sociological analyses. To this end an attempt will be made at the outset of our research on whistleblowing to identify and stipulate its defining features and to distinguish these from common but non-essential features of whistleblowing. This will be done also with an eye to distinguishing the definitional features of whistleblowing from features that are relevant to its justification.

To facilitate this analysis, it will be helpful to begin with several definitions that have been introduced quickly and used carelessly in the literature. Here are four such definitions.

> The employee is said to have "blown the whistle" when, without support or authority from his superiors, he independently makes known concerns to individuals outside the organization (Chalk and von Hippel 1979) [6].

> Whistleblowers sound an alarm from within the very organization in which they work, aiming to spotlight neglect or abuses that threaten the public interest (Bok 1980) [7].

> Whistleblowing is an attempt by a member or former member of an organization to bring illegal or socially harmful activities of the organization to the attention of the public (James 1980) [8].

> Whistleblowers, as we know, are employees who believe their organization is engaged in illegal, dangerous, or unethical conduct. Usually, they try

to have such conduct corrected through inside complaint, but if it is not, the employee turns to
government authorities or the media and makes the
charge public. (Westin 1981) [9].

In order to uncover the meaning of whistleblowing, we
will have to look at how the whistle is blown, who blows the
whistle, and on what the whistle is blown. It may be useful
to begin with a case that roughly fits the definitions just
cited and which, I hope to show, is paradigmatic of whistleblowing.

A PARADIGM CASE

In 1967 John McGee, a middle-level engineer, went to
Bangkok for the Navy Fuel Supply Office (NFSO) to monitor
the delivery of petroleum, oil, and lubricants to Thailand
and South Vietnam. He soon began to complain to his supervisor that huge quantities of petroleum were being stolen for
a well-organized black market because of a lax and corrupt
system of invoice controls. The supervisor refused to do anything about this and told McGee that he would be fired if he
caused any trouble.
McGee wrote the NFSO in Washington requesting that the
monitoring system be investigated, but there was evidently
no response. In the meantime his relationship with his supervisor deteriorated. There was a series of unpleasant exchanges including an official letter of reprimand from the
supervisor to McGee that McGee appealed through NFSO's grievance channels. Finally, McGee received a "resign or be
fired" ultimatum.
Soon after that McGee wrote to Senator William Proxmire
who demanded an investigation by the General Accounting Office. A preliminary report showed that 52 percent of all petroleum deliveries to Thailand had been stolen over a ten-
month period in 1967.[10]

WHISTLEBLOWING AS AN ACTION

We can locate the phenomenon of whistleblowing as an
action. All four of the definitions quoted earlier refer
to individual's doing something. Bok describes whistleblowers as those who "sound an alarm." Westin describes them
as employees who "go to government authorities or the media." But to say that whistleblowing is an action by no

means simplifies matters, for generally there are complex philosophical problems in individuating actions.

Actions can be described and redescribed with what Feinberg has called "the accordian effect,"[11] and the act of blowing the whistle is no exception. In the paradigm case McGee sees and evaluates something, talks to his supervisor, writes memos, ponders and writes a senator. Each one of these activities might be redescribed in an almost infinite number of ways, and any set of these activities might be described as one action. Some subset can be redescribed as "blowing the whistle." The accordian effect is inherent in the way we talk about actions. Mentioning it serves to caution us that whistleblowing is a complex action; its borders cannot always be sharply designated.

More importantly, whistleblowing is an intentional action. One cannot blow the whistle inadvertently or without realizing it. For example, if an agent inadvertently leaves a document damaging to her employer on a restaurant table where a newspaper reporter happens to sit down, read the document, recognize its implications and later publish it, the agent's behavior cannot be called whistleblowing. The agent did not intentionally call public attention to the document. It is, perhaps, due to her that the information is made public, but it is not due to her action.

An agent might act in ways that lead to information being made public, but if the action was not aimed at making the information public, then it seems quite wrong to call it whistleblowing. A real incident illustrates this point. Several years ago an editor of the Los Angeles Herald-Examiner objected when his superiors ordered that color reproductions of master paintings of a Madonna and child be airbrushed so that they would not show the penis of baby Jesus. The editor's efforts to have the decision changed failed, and he resigned believing that the airbrushing was unethical. He then sought employment with the Los Angeles Free Press. When asked why he had resigned from the Herald-Examiner he explained his reasons. The Free Press used this information in an expose satirizing the Herald-Examiner.[12] The editor's action resulted in information (damaging information) about the Herald-Examiner being made public, but the editor's action had not aimed at making the information public. For this reason, it seems wrong to call his action whistleblowing.

In order to rule out cases where information is made public due to accidental or unintentional acts, we will have to stipulate that the individual action involved in whistleblowing must be intended to make information public. But let us keep in mind that intention and motive are not the same. Whistleblowers may have a variety of motives for blowing the whistle. They may be motivated by concerns for the public safety, by desires to get their jobs back, or to be redeemed from accusations made against them. Their motives may be noble or they may be vicious. They may want to see their superiors punished. They may be acting because they have been poorly treated. It would make little sense to distinguish whistleblowing actions from nonwhistleblowing actions on the basis of the motive of the agent. Indeed, since motives are often impossible to determine, it might make the concept of whistleblowing useless. Thus, motives should be considered quite irrelevant to the definition of whistleblowing. Nevertheless, they may be relevant when it comes to justifying an act of whistle blowing, as DeGeorge and Bowie suggest.[13]

Before we state these features in the form of a definition, it should be noted that the whistle may be blown by more than one agent. For example, Holger Hjortsvong, Robert Bruder and Max Blankenzee jointly blew the whistle on the Bay Area Rapid Transit (BART) project.[14] These three men acted jointly in making the defects of the system public, and we refer to their actions as one case of whistleblowing.

Given this discussion, we can now specify the first condition of the act of whistleblowing as occurring when:

1. the individual(s) performs an action or series of actions intended to make information public.

Going Public

The phrase "blowing the whistle" conjures up images of making noise or drawing attention to something. Indeed, as already mentioned, Bok characterizes whistleblowers as those who "sound an alarm." It is certainly not necessary to make noise literally in order to blow the whistle. You may simply write your accusations down and send them to the media. However, the idea of drawing attention to something, or of making something known, seems critical here. All four of the definitions mentioned earlier have this element in one form or another. In addition to Bok's "sounding an alarm," Chalk and von Hippel write of making concerns known, and James writes of bringing activities to the attention of the public. Likewise Westin mentions going to government authorities or the media.

Internal vs. External Dissent

Consider the following nonparadigmatic, hypothetical case: John Crandle works for a large production company. He notices that people working next to him are letting items pass through the assemblyline that do not meet the standards required by law. He reports this to his supervisor, and she says she knows this but wants John to keep quiet about it. The problem persists, so John goes several levels up the management hierarchy and reports the matter to a vice-president. The vice-president responds by firing the supervisor and reprimanding the workers. The problem is settled and neither the vice-president nor John Crandle tell anyone else inside or outside the organization.

Has John Crandle blown the whistle? He has deliberately drawn attention to wrongdoing, but he has not drawn public attention to it. Ordinary usage is not very clear on this point. That is, the phrase "blowing the whistle" is sometimes used to refer to cases where an individual has simply circumvented the formal or normal channels of authority in an organization to report wrongdoing. On the other hand, cases of this kind do not qualify as whistleblowing on three of the definitions cited earlier. Chalk and von Hippel specify that whistleblowers make their concerns known to individuals "outside the organization." Westin specifies that the whistleblower goes to "government authorities or the media," and James claims that whistleblowers attempt to bring activities "to the attention of the public."

For two reasons we insist that only those who go outside the organization should be considered whistleblowers. First, the range of cases in which an individual circumvents normal hierarchical channels is quite broad and diverse. To include all of these in the definition would make whistleblowing a rather general term closer in meaning to "dissent within an organization." More importantly, the deeper issue here has to do with the moral justification of acts of whistleblowing, and from this perspective, acts of circumventing the normal channels of authority are quite different from acts of going outside the organization. From the point of view of the person contemplating an action, it would seem that reasons for going outside the organization must be far weightier than the reasons for going quietly to a superior of one's immediate supervisor. The difference here is due in part to the consequences for the organization. These are likely to be much more serious when one goes outside the organization.

Thus, there is good reason to specify whistleblowing narrowly. Of course, this is not to deny similarities between the two types of cases. In fact we could adopt terminology that recognizes the distinction. For example, we might call those who circumvent channels of authority inside the organization "internal whistleblowers" and those who go outside the organization "external whistleblowers." DeGeorge does something like this. My point is that the distinction between these two kinds of cases is significant and ought to be recognized.

I prefer to reserve the term "whistleblowing" for actions in which the agent goes outside the organization and, thus, will continue to use the term in this way. Because of this, a note of caution is in order. John Crandle is not a whistleblower by my definition because he did not make his concerns known outside the organization. John McGee, on the other hand, is a whistleblower even though he used channels inside the organization. Going to someone inside the organization does not preclude blowing the whistle. Individuals may tell their superiors of their suspicions and later on (or simultaneously) make the information public. Furthermore, while going to a superior does not preclude blowing the whistle, it is not an essential ingredient of blowing the whistle either. In many cases of whistleblowing, as in the case of John McGee, individuals make some attempt to tell someone about their concerns before they go public, but there seems to be no reason to insist that to be a whistleblower one must do this. There may be no one inside the organization who can be trusted. There may be good reason to believe that no good will come from using internal mechanisms. This would, for example, preclude anonymity. Whether or not an individual tries internal mechanisms before going public may be important in justifying cases of whistleblowing, for in some situations it may be morally preferable to seek a remedy without publicity. However, that is a matter of justification, not a matter of definition. Thus, we need not build into the definition of whistleblowing anything about trying internal mechanisms.

Going Outside the Corporation

Now, even if we restrict whistleblowing to those cases where the individual goes outside the organization, we have to designate what we mean more carefully. On the one hand, the borders of an organization are not always clear, especially government organizations. If I work for the Environmental Protection Agency (EPA) and I report wrongdoing in the EPA to the Congress, have I gone outside? Did McGee go "outside" when he contacted the Washington office of NFSO? Furthermore, could someone be said to have blown the whistle if he or she conveyed information to someone outside the organization but insisted that this person keep the information secret? Could someone be said to have blown the whistle if he or she casually mentioned something about wrongdoing at work, to a friend? I would think not.

The number of people one tells is not important here, for whistleblowers often tell only one reporter or one law enforcement official. But whom they tell is significant, as are the conditions they place on the transfer of information. Whistleblowers cannot insist that the information remain secret, nor can they insist that the person told take no action. On the contrary, whistleblowers reveal information to individuals whom they expect to respond by publicizing the information, by investigating it, or by using it to stop an activity or remedy a situation.

It is tempting, then, to side with Westin and stipulate that whistleblowers go to government authorities or to the media. But this will not do either. For one thing, if one works in a government agency, going to a government official may not be going outside. For another, someone might take information to a government official, and if the official does not believe what he or she is told and refuses to investigate further or to relay the information to others, then the person has not succeeded in blowing the whistle. Suppose, for example, that John McGee had gone to another senator and the senator had not believed him and refused to do anything. Suppose further that McGee had become discouraged and taken no further action. Would we say that he had blown the whistle? I think not.

To blow the whistle one must succeed in getting information beyond a single official or reporter. This element of success is, perhaps, represented by the notion of "making something public." That is, by saying that acts of whistleblowing are acts that make information public, we in effect stipulate that whistleblowers are those who succeed in getting the information out. This also has the advantage of leaving open the way in which the information can get out. The whistleblower may contact government authorities, the media, or some private individual who can assist in making the information public. And, of course, this stipulation retains my earlier specification that whistleblowers go outside the organization, for when one goes public, one necessarily goes outside the organization.

Making Information Public

Nevertheless, there is a problem with using the notion "making information public". It is hard to specify what we mean when we say something has been "made public." To be sure, it is tempting to say that it means "widely known." When someone blows the whistle on wrongdoing in an organization, he or she brings it to the attention of a broad range of people. This account would capture what we associate with classic cases of whistleblowing, cases such as BART, where the media transmitted the accusations against BART across the country. Still, how are we to determine what counts as "widely known?" On the one hand, the degree of publicity varies broadly from case to case. Sometimes the whistleblower's accusations are publicized in the national media, sometimes only in local media. Sometimes the whistleblower testifies at a congressional hearing and little reaches the papers. At times whistleblowers give information to law enforcement officials who quietly investigate the situation so that the whistleblower's complaints may never reach the press depending on how the investigation turns out.

Not only does the amount of attention drawn vary, but the attention paid often depends on factors over which the whistleblower has little control. It may depend on the timing of the complaints, the reporter or paper contacted, or public interest in the organization on whom the whistle is blown. Thus, we cannot insist that to be a whistleblower, one must make his or her concern widely known.

We must use some other account of "public", and I believe the key notion here is <u>accessibility</u>. Something that is made public is made accessible to public view. People may not attend to it. They may choose to ignore it, but if they want it, it is there for them. This accessibility is captured with the notion of making something "a matter of public record." Someone may enter something into the public record by having it published in a newspaper, by getting it into the <u>Congressional Record</u> as proceedings of a congressional hearing, as well as by making it so widely known that it is a matter of common knowledge. To say that something is a matter of public record is, in some sense, simply to say that it is not a secret. It is to say that some people know it and others may know it if they look.

If we use this notion of public record, then a person can blow the whistle and not be heard, in the sense that no one may pay particular attention to what has been recorded. However, the whistle has been blown in the sense that the information has been recorded and is now accessible where it was not before. This notion also allows for the case where an individual goes quietly to the FBI or a regulatory agency. If the individual is not believed and nothing happens, the whistle has not been blown; but if an investigation is undertaken, then the person's accusations are in the records of the agency. Whether the agency publicizes the information at all or before or after a long or short investigation is irrelevant. The whistle has been blown.

Using this notion of entering something into the public record, we can now add a second element to our definition.

An act of whistleblowing occurs when:

1. the individual performs an action or series of actions intended to make information public;
2. the information is made a matter of public record.

Now, one caution must be made. Though we have stipulated that to blow the whistle one must succeed in making information public, we have not built the criteria for successful whistleblowing into the definition. The definition of whistleblowing is logically independent of the criteria to be used to judge its success or failure and these will be examined later in this chapter. Up to this point we have merely specified that the whistleblower must succeed in making information a matter of public record to qualify as a whistleblower.

What Is Made Public

We have been using "information" to talk about what is made public, but is this an adequate way to characterize what is made a matter of public record when the whistle is blown? Chalk and von Hippel refer to making "concerns" known. James specifies that whistleblowers bring "illegal or socially harmful activities" to the attention of the public. Westin refers to "illegal, dangerous, or unethical conduct." Bok mentions "neglect or abuses that threaten the public interest." Chalk and von Hippel speak in very general terms of "concerns". The other specifications seem to come closer to identifying what whistleblowers point to—some threat to public interest or as a socially harmful activity. It would seem that we can capture this by use of the general term "wrongdoing." This is general enough to encompass illegal, immoral, and dangerous, and it makes clear that what is reported will not be something an organization wants to be known.

Still there is a problem. Bowie has suggested that whistleblowers be distinguished from tattletales.[15] The latter report trivial infractions such as the use of company stationery for personal letters or the use of four letter words by public officials. Such people are often perceived simply as a nuisance, rarely as praiseworthy. To avoid confusion between the tattletale and the whistleblower, we need to specify that the wrongdoing made public by an act of whistleblowing is nontrivial.

A further problem remains. Often the whistleblower cannot say that something wrong has actually occurred because he or she is trying to prevent the wrong before it happens. In other cases the whistleblower does not know for sure that the wrong is occurring or has occurred, but he or she has some evidence that indicates that it is or has. Whistle-blowers are often relaying beliefs or suspicions rather than facts. For this reason it seems best to refer to what is reported as <u>information</u> and to specify that the information may be <u>about possible or actual wrongdoing</u>.

We should note that whistleblowers have varying degrees of evidence of the wrongdoing they report. Sometimes their concern is based on documents they have seen; sometimes it is based on their expert opinion; and sometimes it is based on something they have witnessed. The amount of evidence they have and their degree of certainty that the wrongdoing did or will occur is important to the justification of particular cases of whistleblowing (as Bowie and DeGeorge point out). Given the harm done to organizations by accusations of wrongdoing, the degree of certainty may tip the scale in justifying whistleblowing. Indeed, other things being equal, the degree of evidence may tip the scale far enough to make whistleblowing obligatory. But the certainty or amount of evidence revealed does not seem relevant to the definition of whistleblowing. As far as the definition goes, we need only say that whistleblowers make public information about possible or actual, nontrivial wrongdoing.

Whistleblowing always takes place in the context of an organization. As the phrase is used, one does not "blow the whistle" on individual behavior--be it illegal, immoral, or threatening to the public--except when that individual behavior is part of an organization's activity. So, the wrongdoing whistleblowers report is always wrongdoing in an organization.

To incorporate these points we can add a third condition to the definition. An act of whistleblowing occurs when:

1. an individual performs an action or series of actions intended to make information public;
2. the information is made a matter of public record;
3. the information is about possible or actual, nontrivial wrongdoing in an organization.

Who Blows the Whistle

Now, we turn to the question of who blows the whistle. So far, we have been talking about whistleblowing as an action. But, of course, actions are performed by agents. Earlier we noted that in the definitions we cited, whistleblowers were characterized as employees or members of organizations on whom they report. Our definition does not yet reflect this.

If I come across information about wrongdoing in an organization that I do not work in, and I deliberately make the information public, I would not be considered a whistleblower. Whistleblowers, as Bok puts it, sound the alarm "from within the very organization in which they work." But must a whistleblower presently be an employee of the organization? James specifies that the whistleblower may be a member or former member of the organization. In fact a number of people who have expressed concerns to other members of an organization about wrongdoing in the organization have been fired. Subsequent to their being fired, they have made their concerns known publicly. Many have also quit because they no longer wanted to be part of the wrongdoing or because they thought their quitting might draw attention to the problem.[16] It would be odd to say that these people are not whistleblowers. One must have a special relationship to the organization, but this can be captured by specifying that the individual be a member or former member.

That the whistleblower is or was a member of the organization is important in part because whistleblowers are often accused by the organization of disloyalty. They are said to violate a duty to their employers. This connotation is not given up by including those who are former members of the organization, for one does not cease to have an obligation to an organization when one ceases to be employed by it. For example, one still has an obligation to keep trade secrets. Thus, we can allow former employees of organizations to count as whistleblowers without losing the connotation of whistleblowers as those who defy their employers.

Stipulating membership or former membership in the organizations allows us to distinguish whistleblowers from those who assist in whistleblowing. For example, newspaper reporters, as well as others like Senator Proxmire or Ralph Nader, call attention to wrongdoing in an organization but are not members of the organization. This feature may be added to our definition by specifying the following condition:

4. the individual who performs the action is a member or former member of the organization.

Too much should not be inferred from this condition, however. In particular, just because whistleblowers are members or former members of the organizations on whom they blow the whistle does not necessarily mean that blowing the whistle is an act of disloyalty. Even if we avoid the hard question of what an employee's duty is to his or her employer, it is quite clear that some acts of whistleblowing may be acts of loyalty. If, for example, the most fundamental goals of an organization are being impeded by wrongdoing in some segment of the organization, then an individual who reports this publicly (perhaps after repeated attempts to let this be known to his or her superiors) is doing a great service to the organization. This is especially evident if we consider civil servants. They work for the government, and when they report wrongdoing in a segment or agency of the government, their acts may be acts of loyalty to the principles and procedures of the government. Since whistleblowing takes place in an organization with many levels of hierarchy, one can be loyal and disloyal at different levels at the same time. Therefore, while acts of whistleblowing have an element of disloyalty (for example to a particular superior or segment of an organization), the situation is usually one of complex loyalties. Condition (4) leaves room for this while still insisting that the whistleblower have a special relationship to the organization, that of member or former member.

We now have a full definition of whistleblowing. An act of whistleblowing occurs when:

1. an individual performs an action or series of actions intended to make information public;
2. the information is made a matter of public record;
3. the information is about possible or actual, nontrivial wrongdoing in an organization;
4. the individual who performs the action is a member or former member of the organization.

A POSSIBLE COUNTEREXAMPLE

Before we turn to questions of success, let us consider a possible counterexample. While working for the Federal Drug Administration, Dr. Carol Kennedy expressed reservations to her peers and superiors about releasing a drug for testing on human subjects. Later she was demoted and transferred. Dissatisfied with the new position, she left the agency. A year or two later she was asked to testify at Senate hearings.[17] She testified willingly and openly. There is no doubt that she expressed dissent and that she was perceived as a threat by her superiors, but it is fairly clear that she did not take the initiative in drawing public attention to the wrongdoing. She was asked to aid someone else in doing this, and she merely did not refuse to help.

Nevertheless, Dr. Kennedy's behavior fits our definition of whistleblowing. She acted when she testified. Her action was intended to make information public. Her testimony, in fact, made information a matter of public record, and the information concerned wrongdoing in an organization of which she was a former member. Should her action be considered whistleblowing?

We are inclined to insist that it is whistleblowing. The locus of initiative in acts of whistleblowing varies so much that we cannot draw a sharp division. Some whistleblowers take the initiative entirely on their own and in isolation. Some do it after discussion with peers who share their concerns. Others do it when they are fired for trying internal mechanisms. Still others do it when it appears that they may be implicated. The degree of initiative that the whistleblower takes varies with the circumstances of the case and the whistleblower's motives, but this does not seem to be something that should be considered part of the definition. Whatever spurred Dr. Kennedy to act, she chose to make her concerns a matter of public record. Thus, her action constitutes blowing the whistle.

A stronger counterexample is provided if we suppose that Dr. Kennedy was not just asked to testify but was subpoenaed. In that case her testimony would seem to be coerced. This would also be the case if a person had been arrested and, through plea bargaining, agreed to give information about some wrongdoing in the organization in which they worked. It is tempting, then, to try to draw a distinction between coerced and uncoerced actions that make information about wrongdoing public. The temptation, however, should be resisted for two reasons. On the one hand, there is not a sharp distinction between coerced and uncoerced actions, but rather a continuum. Thus, the distinction would make the definition less, rather than more, precise. On the other hand, ordinary usage does not seem to justify the distinction. One can easily imagine the media printing something like the following: "In a plea bargaining arrangement, John Doe blew the whistle on Rand Corporation." Ordinary usage does not distinguish coerced revelations from uncoerced whistleblowing.

In refusing to build into the definition of whistleblowing the conditions that motivate the whistleblower to act, we come back to the earlier point about the difference between intention and motive. What the whistleblower aims at with his or her action is much clearer and easier to identify than the motive for his or her action, which will be buried in psychological theory. On this point we diverge from DeGeorge who specifies that whistleblowing (the kind he will talk about) is an act done "for moral reasons." The whistleblower's reasons for acting are relevant to justifying his or her action, but not to categorizing them. For this reason they should be kept out of the definition.

With the definition provided here, the task of determining when acts of whistleblowing are justified should be much easier. The task of studying whistleblowing as a distinct social phenomenon is now possible as well. During the course of the analysis we have also uncovered several factors that might bear on the justification of whistleblowing. These include the reasons for acting, the degree of certainty that the whistleblower has about the wrongdoing, and whether or not the whistleblower has tried to remedy the wrongdoing by internal mechanisms. These factors will bear on our understanding of when whistleblowing is permissible and when it is morally obligatory, but these factors should not be confused with definitional features.

SUCCESSFUL WHISTLEBLOWING

Employees who protest wrongdoing in an organization, whether they do it from within as present employees or from without as former employees, may succeed or fail. How are we to measure their success? Two points of view can be adopted. The first is subjective: Did they achieve what they had in mind? The second is objective: Did others, in some way, heed their warnings? Both perspectives need to be employed for a complete set of criteria for successful whistleblowing.

Raising One's Voice

If one reflects on the metaphor of whistleblowing, one can break the process down into three stages: blowing, making a noise, and being heard. One can succeed or fail at each stage, and one cannot get to the last stage unless one successfully passes through the two earlier stages. The analogy is helpful for clarifying the criteria for successful dissent.

Imagine a child who picks up a whistle, looks at it, plays with it but does nothing more. This child is like the employee who becomes concerned about illegal or immoral corporate practices, frets about what to do, perhaps loses some sleep worrying about it, and decides to do nothing—or more simply and realistically never decides to do something. As a whistleblower this person is a total failure. Indeed, according to the four defining conditions of whistleblowing, this person would not count as a whistleblower at all.

Next consider the child who attempts to blow the whistle, but fails because he or she does not blow hard enough: The child does not make any noise. Likewise, employees may become concerned, talk to their friends or co-workers, but never put enough effort into what they are doing to make any noise. As with the child who huffs and puffs, nothing happens. This person, too, fails at being a whistleblower.

Finally, the child may succeed in making noises, but fail to be heard; no one is listening, or willing to listen. Employees may write memos, contact reporters, call their congressional representatives, and yet nothing happens. Their concerns are dismissed as needless worries or complaints from a disgruntled employee rather than legitimate causes of concern. They are not yet whistleblowers.

This analysis applies to whistleblowing in both its literal and metaphorical senses. An employee can be concerned, fret about a problem, but take no action. The fretting puts one on the track to becoming a whistleblower, but the lack of action precludes the label. Or one can take some action, make a phone call or write a letter, but drop the matter before one has done enough to make a difference. Or finally, one can set out on a course of action designed to correct wrongdoing, but never engage the attention of others; one is misunderstood, dismissed, or just not taken seriously.

To blow the whistle one has to overcome three hurdles:

1. one must become genuinely concerned with wrongdoing and take positive steps toward voicing one's concerns;
2. one must put sufficient effort into alerting others that one sounds the alarm that something is wrong;
3. one's message must be sufficiently loud and clear that it is correctly heard by others.

If all three conditions are satisfied, then one has successfully voiced one's concerns. But this is only the first phase and satisfies the subjective point of view.

Getting Action

Various responses from others are possible, depending on several factors such as the concerns voiced, the organization involved, the people addressed, the evidence gathered, the strategy adopted, and the solutions available. Whereas the three criteria listed previously represent individually necessary and jointly sufficient conditions for successfully voicing one's concerns, any one of the following responses may bring success or failure. For this reason it is difficult to judge a whistleblower's success conclusively and with any finality.

This ambiguity is compounded by a causal problem. How can we isolate the individual's action and determine how much effect it alone had? We cannot and therefore we cannot say with certainty that the subsequent changes were due to the actions of the whistleblower--and no one or nothing else. Because an individual's actions are filtered through a social network and mediated by the actions of others, objective success is difficult to determine.

Nevertheless, we can identify four outcomes, each of which would count as a measure of success.

A Change of Policy

One's protests are objectively successful if corporate practices are changed. If one is concerned with past wrong-doing, one obviously cannot change it: the past is past and as such unalterable. But one can change the policies or procedures that allowed or caused the past wrong to occur and thereby reduce the likelihood of similar wrongs in future.

Compensation to Victims

One can redress past injustices by compensating the victims. Doing so does not change the past wrongs, but it does reduce their net harm. It may also serve as a deterrent to others if the organization must pay the compensation.

Diminished Risk

No wrong may yet have occurred, but may be likely to occur in the near future. One has achieved a measure of success if the probability of its occurring or recurring is diminished. This reduction in possible harm may take the form of informing the pubic about risks so that they can take steps to avoid jeopardizing their health or safety. Or it may take the form of a new corporate practice that places the public less at risk.

A Careful Investigation

It may turn out that the prior assessment of the risk, though reasonable given the evidence at the time, is incorrect. New findings may show that the harm is less likely, the danger more remote, or the wrong far less serious. If the worries were reasonable and the new evidence reliable, then to disprove these worries is a measure of success. A balanced, responsible, and thorough inquiry that alleviates reasonable concerns constitutes a measure of success.

SEVEN STRATEGIES FOR SUCCESS

Professionals can use any one (or more) of several strategies to address wrongdoing within their organization. Not all of these strategies are available to every employee, and some may work for one person and in one situation, but not another. Given that the whistleblower must go outside the organization, the first group are not strategies for blowing the whistle but, more generically, strategies for dealing with dissent in the workplace.

Internal Channels

First, employees can work through the regular chain of command to bring the issue to the attention of senior management, who have the authority to address the problem. These channels may take the form of a corporate ombudsman, grievance procedures or informal consultations. Both formal meetings and informal bull sessions can effectively address and resolve problems.

Community Groups

Second, they can go outside the organization to enlist the support of members of the community. When a dispute is not resolved within the organization, they may have recourse to sympathetic, organized citizens in the community at large. A well-informed and well-situated community leader offers the prospect of bringing to bear external pressure that will lead to a change that the employee was unable to bring about by internal means.

Congressional Committees

Third, individuals can take their message to Congress or an appropriate committee. Bringing an issue to the attention of government officials, elected to represent and safeguard the interests of society generally, may provide the publicity and pressure to bring about corporate action.

The Media

Fourth the individual can call a newspaper, radio station, magazine, or television station. A sympathetic reporter can disseminate information outside the organization to people in power or to a grass roots political group.

The Courts

Fifth, the individual can sue. The courts are a legal channel of redress. In addition to publicizing the case, such a strategy can bring legal pressure to bear and force action on the organization, especially when an individual's legal rights have been violated or a governmental regulation disregarded.

Professional Societies

Sixth, individuals can go to their professional associations, and solicit the support of their peers. The concerted efforts of an organized group of professionals can bring about a change that one person alone could not secure.

The Inspectors General

Seventh, an employee in the federal government can go to the office of the inspector general. This official serves as a governmental watchdog, monitoring waste and corruption in federal agencies and protecting those who disclose it.

THE CRITERIA FOR SUCCESS

How can one appraise these different strategies? The success of each can be judged against four criteria.

Informing Others

Just as in whistleblowing one can ask whether others heard the whistle, one can ask of each strategy whether it allowed the individual to voice his or her concerns effectively. One critical question is: Did others become aware of the problems? This question is an epistemological one. It asks whether the flow of information was successful, whether the beliefs were communicated. Failure means that the facts were distorted, key bits of information omitted, or the problem misinterpreted.

Mobilizing Resources

Second, one can ask whether the dispute was taken seriously. Did the individuals or groups contacted mobilize their resources in response, or did the whistleblower's protests fall on deaf ears? To the extent that others are moved to act in a deliberate and responsible way--either to investigate the wrongdoing or correct it--the whistleblower has succeeded.

Changing Corporate Conduct

Third, the use of a strategy will be successful if it leads to a change in the organization's behavior or policies. If the whistleblower's objections are warranted, the organization should respond responsibly and change the actions or procedures that led to the wrongdoing. If the whistleblower's judgment was mistaken, the organization may want to institute measures that will provide for a less costly and more direct means of addressing the issues. Some mechanism for dealing with dissent within the organization would obviate the need to go outside it.

Reconciling Differences

Fourth and finally, whistleblowing will be successful if dissent is diminished. If the disagreement was rooted in reasonable but mistaken factual assumptions, correcting these mistakes will resolve it. If the disagreement was rooted in conflicting value judgments, the most one can achieve is a tolerance for these differences and a just procedure for resolving conflicts internally.

CONCLUSION

This chapter has sought to determine what whistleblowing is and how it can be judged a success. A definition was developed using a paradigm case that distinguished it from similar but distinct actions and criteria were set forth for assessing the success of the whistleblower's actions. In the course of this discussion several distinct strategies for dealing with dissent in the workplace were identified.

But why does whistleblowing occur? What are the features of individuals or organizations that make whistleblowing likely? To answer these questions we need a general theory of organizational behavior from which we can generate hypotheses about the occurrence of whistleblowing.

NOTES

*The first portion of this introductory chapter, dealing with the definition of whistleblowing, was written by Dr. Deborah Johnson. She served as project associate. We are grateful to her for permission to reprint it.

1. See, for example, Jack Anderson, "Fitzgerald Vendetta: Another Chapter," Washington Post, November 1, 1980; Mike Causey, "VA Whistle Blowers Win Transfer Stays," Washington Post, April 8, 1980; John M. Credson, "Former FBI Agent Tells Investigators of Widespread Abuse and Corruption," New York Times, January 20, 1979, p. 8; Philip Greer and Myron Kanel, "It Doesn't Pay to Blow the Whistle on Hollywood Crime," Los Angeles Daily Journal, January 31, 1980; Rich Jaroslovsky, "Blowing the Whistle Begins a Nightmare for Lawyer Joe Rose," Wall Street Journal, November 9, 1977; "Senate Panel Hears Testimony by Two G.S.A. Whistleblowers," New York Times, June 24, 1978, p. 1.

2. See for example, Andrew Baran, "Federal Employment—The Civil Service Reform Act of 1978—Removing Incompetents and Protecting Whistle Blowers," Wayne Law Review 26 (1979): 97-118.

3. For a complete listing of the literature, see James Bowman, Frederick Elliston and Paula Lockhart, Professional Dissent: An Annotated Bibliography and Resource Guide (New York: Garland, 1983).

4. See Alan Westin, Whistle-Blowing: Loyalty and Dissent in the Corporation (New York: McGraw-Hill, 1981); and Ralph Nader, et al., Whistle Blowing: The Report of the Conference on Professional Responsibility (New York: Grossman Publishers, 1972).

5. William Saphire, Political Dictionary.

6. Rosemary Chalk and Frank von Hippel, "Due Process for Dissenting Whistle-Blowers" Technology Review (June-July (1979): 49-55.

7. Sissela Bok, "Whistleblowing and Professional Responsibility" New York University Education Quarterly 10 (Summer 1980): 2-10.

8. Gene G. James, "Whistle Blowing: Its Nature and Justification" Philosophy In Context 10 (1980): 99-117.

9. Alan F. Westin, Whistle-Blowing: Loyalty and Dissent in Corporations (New York: McGraw-Hill, 1981).

10. See Charles Peters and Taylor Branch, Blowing the Whistle (New York: Praeger, 1972).

11. Joel Feinberg, Doing & Deserving: Essays in the Theory of Responsibility (Princeton: Princeton University Press, 1970).
12. Martin Malin, "Protecting the Whistleblower from Retaliatory Discharge," Journal of Law Reform, 16:2 (1983): 289.
13. See their contributions to Conflicting Loyalties in the Workplace, ed. F. A. Elliston (Notre Dame: University of Notre Dame Press, 1985).
14. Anderson, et al., Divided Loyalties: Whistle-Blowing at BART (West Lafayette, IN: Purdue Research Foundation, 1980).
15. Norman Bowie, Business Ethics (Englewood Cliffs, NJ: Prentice-Hall, 1982).
16. Vivian Weil, "The Three G.E. Engineers," in Conflicting Loyalties in the Workplace, ed. F. A. Elliston (Notre Dame: University of Notre Dame Press, 1985).
17. Carol Kennedy, "Dissent Can Be Dangerous," Medical Dimensions 7 (May 1978): 25-27.

TWO
THEORIES AND
HYPOTHESES

Whistleblowing or, to use the more inclusive term, professional dissent, can be examined from a number of theoretical perspectives.[1] It will be the goal of this chapter to explore the three major ones: individual, organizational and environmental. All three are crucial to our assessment of the subject because any one provides only a limited view. This chapter will establish a comprehensive theoretical framework that identifies and explains the pertinent factors and elaborates hypotheses for further research.

INDIVIDUAL PERSPECTIVES

Whistleblowing can be examined from the perspective of individual employees who find themselves caught between the conflicting demands of their employers and their own consciences. Four theories bear upon the situation from an individual perspective: personal characteristics or traits, individual role; process-symbolic interaction; and labeling theory.[2]

Personal Trait Theory

Is there something common to the personality structure of whistleblowers that separates them from other employees? Or is a whistleblower just like any other employee, but caught in a tough situation? Given the hurdles that must be overcome to succeed at blowing the whistle (see Chapter One), it might be expected that whistleblowers must be relatively strong-minded and strong-willed individuals. Whistleblowing is a "political" act committed by an employee who has the fortitude to go beyond the established system of organizational power and control.

Whistleblowers must have relatively high ideals and staunch principles to warrant jeopardizing or sacrificing a promising career. Unlike other employees, they feel a strong obligation to "take action" rather than compromise their standards by remaining silent. The following hypothesis summarizes this presumption.

Hypothesis 1: Whistleblowers are strong-minded and strong-willed individuals with high ideals and moral principles.

Whistleblowers might also be regarded as conscientious employees who identify closely with their organization. They may be committed workers who are especially dedicated to the explicit goals of their company, taking their roles and responsibilities very seriously. The act of whistleblowing indicates that they care for the organization. Their more apathetic and less committed coworkers merely put in their time and try not to "rock-the-boat."

Hypothesis 2: Whistleblowing is more likely to occur if individuals are (a) committed to the formal goals of their organization or to the successful completion of their project; (b) identify with the organization; and (c) have a strong sense of professional responsibility.

Process and Symbolic Interaction Theory

Whistleblowing can also be examined from the perspective of interaction theory.[3] This theory would interpret whistleblowing not as a single act but as a series of actions and reactions, much like the accordian effect referred to in Chapter One. As such, whistleblowing is a process that does not happen all at once but unfolds over time. It grows, develops, and acquires a history. Although one stage may be a necessary antecedent to another, the chain of events need not be wholly determined by prior events. Whistleblowing emerges out of a process where practices are observed, questioned, discussed and corrective action proposed, rejected, affirmed, and eventually undertaken. No one could easily predict at the outset what the outcome will be. The process takes on distinct features according to the personality of the participants, the contingencies of the circumstances, and the unanticipated responses of others.

Interaction theory emphasizes the situational components. The way the whistleblowing incident develops depends upon contingencies such as the personalities of the participants, the perspectives through which they view it, and the way they and others respond.

Whistleblowing itself is the final stage of a process that begins in an awareness of an illegal, dangerous or unethical activity within the organization. It grows and takes shape through discussions with coworkers to clarify one's initial worries. If the individual's assessment is confirmed, the individual may begin to seek a way to address the problem through channels within the organization. If these fail, the employee confronts the option of going outside the corporation to redress wrongdoing.

Hypothesis 3: The process of whistleblowing begins when an individual or small group: (a) independently observes illegal, inefficient or unethical practices within their organization; (b) perceives at least tacit support for the validity of their technical analysis of the problem; and (c) perceives the organization to be unresponsive to their concerns.

Symbolic interaction theory emphasizes that human beings relate to the world around them through conventions.[4] People act toward things on the basis of the meanings they have for them. Whistleblowing occurs because an employee has interpreted an event as warranting a response. Their interpretation arises out of social interactions with fellow employees, peers, superiors, and subordinates. Symbolic interaction theory emphasizes that meanings are constructed in and modified through an interpretative process in dealings with people and things. The troubled employee enters into a process of defining and redefining the situation and events as they unfold--frequently coming to see himself or herself as a whistleblower only in retrospect. The employee sizes up situations and tries to make sense of them according to his or her self-understanding inclinations and social responses.

Symbolic interaction theory emphasizes the variety of perspectives that individuals hold. Each interprets the situation from a different angle in terms of his or her own needs, values, and experiences. Each develops a "cognitive map" of the physical and social terrain that serves as a guide for action. To understand why one individual decides to blow the whistle while another does not, one must understand their "cognitive maps"--their system of meaning for understanding their place in the corporate world.

Labeling Theory

After going public, whistleblowers are often "labeled" or "stigmatized." The stigma may be modest: a reduction in organizational status and power. Or it may be extreme: the employee may be called a traitor and condemned to corporate death--fired. They are seen as "deviants" who separated themselves from the loyal members of the organization. Those in authority tend to react negatively to the person rather than to the principle because disloyal employees threaten the group's identity and cohesion. The "stigma" attached to them is deeply discrediting.[5] Somehow they must work out an accommodation to this stain on their identity.

In the early stages whistleblowers are isolated from their coworkers and colleagues physically and psychologically. They are made to feel that they have acted in a reckless, unconscionable and disloyal manner for which they deserve to be demoted, transferred, outlawed, or fired. Close colleagues or coworkers remove themselves from contact. They are seen as contaminated, and others risk the wrath of the organization if they are too sympathetic.

Hypothesis 4: After going public, whistleblowers are "labeled" or stigmatized by their organization and may experience a reduction in organizational status and power if they are not fired.

Personal characteristics or trait theory, process and symbolic interaction theory, and labeling theory approach the subject of whistleblowing from an individual perspective. It is important now to turn to the organizational perspective for a complementary and more comprehensive view.

ORGANIZATIONAL PERSPECTIVE

The organizational perspective is important because individuals do not live or act in a vacuum. The corporation is the most immediate and powerful social context for understanding whistleblowing. Individuals act in response to the requirements of their environment. The large bureaucratic organization is the most common work environment today.[6] Since whistleblowing is an action taken by an employee against the organization, the nature of the organization itself is a factor. Do some have features that make whistleblowing more likely to occur? Do they have ways of dealing with dissent that make whistleblowing less likely? Several features of organizations are pertinent to answering these questions: role definitions, systems/control, organizational culture, work groups, organizational size, technology, and change.

Role Theory

A role consists of typified responses to typified expectations. It involves the anticipation of definite behavior, emotions, and attitudes.[7] The bureaucratic organization consists of a system of roles graded by an authority structure. Individuals must adapt to such a system of roles if they are to remain within the organization. Through formal and informal socialization processes, employees learn, acceptable standards and behavior patterns to be exhibited for the various roles they will be playing and responding to within the organization. The roles individuals play will form, shape, and pattern them and their actions in the organization. Roles range from the very specific and limited to the more general and diffuse. In all cases, however, the role player "fills" the role and enjoys a degree of latitude in adapting the role to his or her own personality.

In large organizations roles become specialized and limited to a relatively isolated aspect of the organization's total activities. Those playing unusual or atypical roles develop an insularity from other role players. They become preoccupied with their own concerns and tend not to acquire insights into the interrelationships of roles and the various perceptions of role players outside their own area of expertise and responsibility. Conflicts arise out of such interrole differences--discrepancies among the various definitions of a role.

In many organizations professionals occupying technical roles have vast knowledge and understanding of highly specialized fields outside the experience and education of their managers. A form of alienation or distance arises between the managers and the professionals due to this organizational specialization of roles. Conflicts and tensions are more likely to occur in large-scale organizations employing professionals since organizational needs and professional requirements often come into conflict.[8] Bureaucratic organizations require predictable behavior, coordination of activities and loyalty. Yet professionals often believe that their authority should be based on their expertise, that they should be free from external control and allowed to exercise their sense of social responsibility.

Managerial expediency can all-too-easily substitute for professional expertise. When this happens, problems arise for which whistleblowing is one solution. It is especially tempting for professionals who have specialized knowledge about a potentially dangerous technical problem neglected by management who pressure them to go on as always. The potential whistleblowers' unquestioning acceptance of the graded system of roles encourages them to leave the decision making to management, while they pursue the job for which they were hired. Dissent is thereby silent.

Hypothesis 5: Whistleblowing is a response by professionals who have knowledge about a potentially dangerous technical problem they see neglected by management and who feel powerless to influence the formal decision-making processes in the organization.

A generalized, in contrast to a specialized, role allows the individual to take note of a much broader range of organizational interactions. Conflicts and questionable practices are more easily observed. Whistleblowing is more likely to occur with individuals occupying such roles. Specialists can more easily occupy themselves with more clearly defined and limited areas of responsibility. The managerial role conveys a sense of authority and responsibility that is not characteristic of a technical role and brings with it a greater measure of autonomy.

Hypothesis 6: Whistleblowing is more likely to occur in organizational roles that are general and diffuse and allow for more autonomy or managerial discretion than in specialized and fragmented roles limited to technical responsibility.

In addition to their organizational role, professionals generally belong to societies of their peers and colleagues. Their self-image and self-concept are often attached to membership within a professional association. They may be expected to identify more with those who share their professional interests, training, and experience. These peers become the "significant others" or "reference groups" to whom they refer when making assessments or judgments on questions of professional concern.[9]

Hypothesis 7: Professionals are more likely to blow the whistle on a nonprofessional or those who belong to another profession due to their sense of professional identification and loyalty.

Blowing the whistle on members of one's own profession might be thought to be easier if the other professionals were not one's close associates but strangers with whom one had little or no previous contact. One might expect conflicts with close colleagues to be worked out through informal channels, whereas such conflict-reduction methods are less available or unavailable when people are more distant.

Hypothesis 8: Blowing the whistle on members of one's own profession would be expected to be easier to do if they were not friends but strangers with whom one had little or limited personal contacts.

Organizational role players associating on a relatively frequent basis establish modes of accommodation unavailable to others who are not regularly or closely in contact with each other.

Hypothesis 9: Blowing the whistle on role players with whom one does not directly associate on the job would be easier than with role players one works with on an intimate, daily basis.

Role congruence generally occurs when there is no conflict between one's professional role and one's role in an organization. It should be recognized that a role allows for a certain degree of latitude in meeting established norms and expectations. An individual will generally attempt to balance competing expectations by adapting and compromising. Yet there are times when individuals face conflicting role expectations within themselves, or between themselves and other role players.[10] For example, employees might feel a strong allegiance to the code of ethics of their professional organization and yet feel that as a loyal employee they must obey the decisions made by their superiors. When a conflict arises between these two expectations, whistleblowing is one solution.

Hypothesis 10: Whistleblowing is more likely when a role incumbent cannot find a compromising position that satisfies conflicting role expectations.

Whistleblowing is more likely if there is consensus among others in the organization about the importance and seriousness of the issue raised. The mutual feeling that management was being unreasonable and unmovable in their decision not to heed the warning would lend further weight to the possibility of blowing the whistle. In this case there would be intrarole consensus (among professionals), and interrole conflict (between professionals and management).[11] The professionals would feel that the situation required a breaching of their typical role duties and a more direct involvement in the decision-making processes since a dangerous situation was being neglected. Management, on the other hand, might tend to see this as a threat to their authority and a breaching of their role expectations of professionals as employees hired for a certain task and not involved with managerial prerogatives.

Hypothesis 11: Whistleblowing is most likely to occur when there is intrarole consensus (agreement on expectations of role behavior by role incumbents) and interrole dissension (nonagreement on expectations of role behavior by nonrole incumbents).

One way to avoid such role conflicts is to blow the whistle anonymously. Going public by name puts a great deal of pressure on a whistleblower. He or she becomes a focal point of public discord, and this attention can adversely affect one's career. By remaining anonymous the individual incurs less risk of reprisals.

Hypothesis 12: Whistleblowing is more likely when the individual can remain anonymous and need not go public by name.

Whistleblowing might be examined as a new role arising from within an organization but transcending its official boundaries. Emergent or newly developing roles may diverge from the official prescribed role system. Organizations with changing, dynamic environments frequently have to respond in innovative ways, and new roles might formally or informally develop to facilitate innovation. Matrix organizations exhibit relatively new and formally chosen role systems that allow greater flexibility in changing dynamic environments. Whistleblowing might be an example of an informally developed role that has arisen in response to conflicting obligations that are not adequately addressed through the official formal role systems.

Systems/Control Theory

Professor Herbert Simon has offered one of the most useful and authoritative definitions of bureaucratic organizations. He sees them as adaptive systems with physical, personal, and social components held together by a network of communications and the willingness of their members to strive toward a common goal. Each organization consists of several subsystems. These range over the technological subsystem consisting of those elements of an organization required for task performance; the structural subsystem that refers to the way in which tasks of an organization are differentiated and integrated; the goals and values subsystem that concerns the mission of the organization, its objectives, and the underlying values; the psychological subsystem that governs interactions between individuals and groups; and finally, the managerial subsystem that coordinates and integrates the others.[12]

As systems, organizations are rationally designed entities whose basic purpose is to survive by supplying products or services to society over an extended period of time. Natural and human resources are sought by the organization to engage in carefully designed activities that result in products or services sold or dispensed to an interested public.

Rensis Likert, an organizational psychologist, has developed a typology of organizations that can be brought to bear upon whistleblowing.[13] He interprets organizations as systems lying on a continuum from exploitative/autocratic (System-I) to participative/democratic (System-4).

System-I is characterized by authoritarian leadership and management: decisions are routinely made at the top and employees are expected to follow them in a largely unquestioning manner. In this type of organization, management places almost no trust in subordinates whom they feel need careful watching and supervision. Motivation is typically secured through fear, threats, and punishment, while communication usually flows in an exclusively downward direction. Goals and controls are set at the top with minimal input from those at lower levels.

System-2 is a benevolent/autocratic type of organization with leadership showing confidence in subordinates. Motivation is secured through rewards and sometimes punishment, while communication flows mostly downward. Policy and decision making is found at the top, although some delegation occurs. Goal setting is determined by issuing orders with occasional invitations from subordinates to make comments. Organizational control is found mostly at the top.

System-3 is a consultative/democratic type of organization. Substantial confidence and trust is placed in subordinates. Motivation occurs through rewards (and occasionally punishment) or involvement. Communication flows vertically and decision-making involves broad policy set at the top but with more delegation present than in System-I or System-2. Goals are set after discussing them with subordinates, and there is a moderate degree of delegation of organizational control.

At the far end of the continuum are System-4 organizations. They are characterized by participative and democratic leadership. A great deal of confidence and trust is shown subordinates. Individuals are typically motivated by rewards and involvement. Communication flows vertically and horizontally, and decisions are made throughout the entire organization. Except in crisis situations, goals are set by group action, and control and review functions are widely shared throughout the organization.

Organizations approximating System-I types tend to have an environment where concerns cannot be raised and addressed at the appropriate level in the organization. The ability to share in organizational control is quite limited. Individual employees are socialized into a firmly established and routinized chain of command and authority system. Unquestioning obedience is expected. Managers tend not to "rock the boat", seek compliance of their subordinates, and prefer to keep "problems" from ascending to their superiors. Threats of demotion, negative performance evaluations, and the use of rewards and punishments can be used to keep the conscience-ridden employee quiet. Jobs are often highly specialized and the role of the professional is to supply a service to management. Whistleblowing might be more probable in this type of organization since dissidents might find their concerns met with stiff resistance and reproach.

On the other hand, organizations approximating the System-4 types would have more opportunities for dissidents to raise questions and issues and share in organizational control. Employees would participate in decision-making and would be able to communicate views freely without threat. Thus whistleblowing, as an extreme act of going outside the organization, is less likely to arise because concerns are more likely to be adequately dealt with within such a democratic and participative environment.

Hypothesis 13: Whistleblowing is more likely to occur in organizations that are closer to System-I (exploitative/autocratic) than System-4 (participative/democratic).

Organizations can also be examined in terms of the chain of command. In tall organizations there is an extensive hierarchy ranging from the top to the bottom of the organization. The structure of power is typically distributed along hierarchical lines with control and decision making centered at the top. In flat organizations, on the other hand, the hierarchy has been reduced to a minimum with upper and lower levels of the organization relatively close. The chain of command is more evenly spread with control and decision-making relatively decentralized and shared. In such organizations individuals would have more opportunity to raise issues and exert influence on the control system. This influence would be more difficult to achieve in taller, more hierarchical organizations.

Hypothesis 14: Whistleblowing is more likely in organizations characterized by hierarchical and centralized control systems than in those with less hierarchical, more decentralized control systems.

Organizational Culture

Organizational culture is a body of common understanding that is manifest in acts, actions, and artifacts and persists through tradition.[14] Each organization can be examined as a society in miniature, with its distinct way of life. There appears to be a dominant managerial culture that most corporate executives in the United States share in--at least to some degree. This dominant culture is typically based on such values as economic efficiency, organizational growth, loyalty to the system, and camaraderie.

It should be recognized, however, that there are differences in the corporate cultures of U.S. organizations. Each organization is unique to itself and possesses a different value and normative system. Occasionally such cultures become dysfunctional: they threaten the survival and well-being of the organization. This is especially true in times of dynamic change such as today.

Whistleblowing might be expected to occur more often in organizations whose culture emphasized such values as economic efficiency, corporate growth, and extreme loyalty to the system, while downplaying attention to questionable practices and unethical behavior on the part of individuals in the organization. The dissident is seen as engaging in "unproductive" activity and creating problems for the immediate welfare of the organization.

The educational and work experience of many individuals in the corporate world is often technical and has not involved a serious examination of ethics and values as they might relate to corporate activity. For this reason, individuals who might see themselves as extremely ethical might not be able to make the connection to their possible unethical behavior within the context of the organization where they work. The individual might see himself or herself as merely following orders—as a "good" employee should when questionable practices occur. This individual would be rewarded along with others for not "rocking the boat" and would witness the sanctions brought to bear on those who fail to go along with the established corporate value and normative system.

Hypothesis 15: Whistleblowing is more likely to occur in organizations whose culture emphasizes economic efficiency, accountability, growth and loyalty to the system while downplaying attention to questionable practices and unethical behavior on the part of its members.

It is important to be aware of the large gap between a personal and social ethic. As L.L. Barnard said many years ago: one can be a good man in a bad situation.[15] Both the most principled manager and the most ethical whistleblower may be conforming to admirable personal codes, yet both codes may be irrelevant or threatening to the organization.

On the other hand, organizations might be sacrificing their long-term welfare for short-run gains by holding tight to their traditional corporate culture. An employee who blows the whistle might initially seem a nuisance. Yet, the whistleblowers may serve as change masters for corporations seeking greater public esteem. The prospect of negative images has been a major issue as corporations struggle against a decline in public confidence and respect. In our electronic age, whistleblowers may safeguard the corporate image which is critical for long-term survival.

It is possible for the corporate culture to be examined and ultimately changed. The influence of top management is obviously a major factor in such a change. The basic values and norms set by top management inevitably have an impact on the entire organization. If unethical practices and questionable behavior is condoned or overlooked by the upper echelon of the organization, those below can be expected to follow suit. In this case whistleblowing would be likely to increase, for conscientious employees would have to go outside the organization for help. But if top management introduces change into the corporate culture by placing greater emphasis on rewarding employees who report unethical practices and questionable activities, whistleblowing might be expected to decrease. In such circumstances the internal values and mechanism for resolving dissent would allow employees to voice their concerns freely and openly to responsible and interested figures in the organization.

Hypothesis 16: If top management does not value and reward employees who report unethical and questionable practices, whistleblowing is more likely to occur.

Corporate culture holds great promise as a useful tool for examining whistleblowing. Too often the focus on individual behavior fails to recognize that this behavior is a function of one's cultural framework. The culture of the corporation inevitably has an impact on the behavior of its members--including whistleblowing behavior.

Work Groups

Work groups have great influence on individuals in the organization. Individual behavior is directly related to the expectations and normative structure of the groups one works in or refers to.[16] Such groups include both the formal ones to which individuals are assigned as well as the informal ones that spontaneously arise out of mutual interests. These groups can be supportive of whistleblowing by confirming individuals' suspicions and by giving them help in direct or indirect ways.

On the other hand, the work group can act as a barrier. If questionable practices have been sustained over a period of time and the group has willingly gone along with it, the individual who raises embarrassing questions stands a good chance of being ridiculed and ultimately ostracized by the work group.

Hypothesis 17: Whistleblowing is more likely to occur when the work group accepts and agrees with the whistleblower's technical assessment and provides emotional support in deciding to blow the whistle.

Organizational Size

The larger the organization the more cumbersome it tends to become. The chain of command becomes removed from individual influence. With a high degree of specialization, responsibility is widely diffused and alienation and discontent increased. Small-scale organizations tend to be more personable, and the concerns of the individual can be more effectively addressed and resolved.

Hypothesis 18: Whistleblowing is more likely in large-scale rather than small-scale organizations.

Organizational Technology

Organizations vary in terms of the technological complexity of their tasks. As work becomes more specialized, the individual worker plays a less important part in the whole. The worker becomes focused on the demands of a particular, isolated and segmented task with little sense of the whole. In such cases management assumes increasing power and control over decision-making, for one of its major goals is to see that the variety of tasks are properly monitored and integrated. In such circumstances professionals have fewer opportunities to voice their concerns about their work or the results of their work that go beyond their immediate task environment.[17]

Hypothesis 19: Whistleblowing is more likely in organizations with technologically complex tasks than in those with less technologically complex tasks.

Organizational Change

Whistleblowing can be examined as a relatively new form of organizational behavior directed toward organizational change. Etzioni's theory of societal guidance can shed some light on organizational change.[18] His theory proposes that there is a difference between control and guidance in change situations. Change cannot be seen simply and exclusively as the result of the dictates of those in positions of authority or control. The direction of change in an organizational system is only partially determined by management. The other sources are found within internal and external processes that interact with the formal control system. Such processes might include the external environments in which organizations act as well as internal environments and the structure of the organization itself. When examining the internal and external environments of organizations, political rather than rational decision-making models are more fruitful for understanding organizational behavior.[19]

Whistleblowing can be seen as a form of organizational guidance through nonformal channels of influence within and outside of the organization. Whistleblowing is an attempt to bring pressure to bear on an organization the employee sees as neglecting the damage it causes the external environment. The whistleblower goes public when he or she feels that the formal inside channels have been exhausted. It is a political act that seeks to right a power imbalance.

It is also an attempt at boundary spanning. The whistleblower tries to forge a link to connect the inside and outside of the organization. It can serve not only to control a powerful organization, but help it adapt more effectively to increasingly dynamic and complex environments.

Hypothesis 20: Whistleblowing is a form of organizational guidance that attempts to span organizational boundaries and change the relationship between the organization and its environment.

Those in leadership positions in bureaucratic organizations might take a more proactive approach to whistleblowing. Often the drive for productivity and greater organizational control threatens to stifle creativity and innovation. Some have argued for institutionalizing whistleblowing as a formal and accepted activity in organizations. If channels were provided for dissent outside the formal control system, the need for the individual to blow the whistle by going to external groups might be obviated.

Hypothesis 21: Whistleblowing will be more likely in organizations that do not provide for dissent within or outside their formal control system.

The preceding has been an attempt to examine whistleblowing from an organizational perspective. The topics have included role theory, systems/control theory, organizational culture, work groups, organizational size and technology, and organizational change. A number of hypotheses have been proposed that need further empirical verification. It is now important to examine organizations in relationship to the external environments in which they function.

ENVIRONMENTAL PERSPECTIVE

Organizations, like individuals, do not exist in a vacuum. They are tied to their environments. It is helpful to examine whether there are any particular organizational environments that are more likely to encourage whistleblowing. The discussion below will explore three pertinent factors: the relationship between the organization and its environment, forces in the environment, and types of environments.

The Organization and its Environment

Any bureaucratic organization is a product of its environment. It was created at a certain time through the sanctions of society and must serve some useful social purpose if it is to prosper or even survive. Organizations can be viewed as systems that implement environmentally imposed goals.[20] All features and characteristics of organizations, including whistleblowing, arise out of a particular historical period characterized by a variety of social processes. Dealing with whistleblowing and whistleblowers is a relatively new problem for organizations that will require a more informed understanding of its nature and roots.

An organization is dependent on its environment in many respects. It must seek there the resources it needs to function such as money, materials and people. It must supply others with desired goods or services that are in demand in the external environment and subsequently purchased.

Organizations depend upon the legitimacy granted them by society. Whistleblowing is a clear and forceful challenge to this legitimacy. It sensitizes those in the external environment to possible dangers arising from illegitimate and unwarranted activities by members of the organization.

On the other hand organizations can be examined as functionally autonomous systems that impose internally determined goals on their environments.[21] The rise of powerful multinational corporations requires a new evaluation of political control systems that transcends the nation-state. Perhaps the most useful way of examining organizations, however, construes them as adaptive open systems that interact with their environment as both shapers and shaped.[22] As open systems, organizations must adapt to their environments by creating boundary positions on the input and output sides. Such boundary positions can sensitize the organization to conflicts and changes and allow for a more effective adaptive response. The ultimate success of the organization can be measured only by its ability to adapt continually to the changing environment in an effective life-preserving manner.

Hypothesis 22: Whistleblowers occupy "unofficial" boundary spanning positions that enable them to point out matters of concern for the organization's relationship to its external environment.

Forces in the Environment

The Rate of Scientific and Technological Change

A number of forces in the organization's external environment bear on whistleblowing. One of the major factors influencing organizational environments today is the rate of scientific and technological change. Alvin Toffler, John Naisbitt and others have examined the effects of rapid technological change on individuals and organizations.[23] As complex new technologies are created and scientific breakthroughs occur in computers, genetics, communications, robotics and other areas, it becomes increasingly difficult for organizations to monitor and integrate them. Inevitably social, legal and moral problems arise about the safety and appropriateness of technical innovations and applied scientific findings.

Hypothesis 23: Whistleblowing is more likely with rapid, new scientific and technological developments.

Economic Conditions

The forces of the marketplace and the emphasis on increasing profit margins, return on investment, and market share have an impact on organizational behavior. This is especially true in "tight" economic times when questions of ethics and social responsibility get pushed to the side as the struggle to survive takes precedence.

Hypothesis 24: Whistleblowing is more likely to occur when the economy is deteriorating or stagnating rather than in times of economic prosperity and growth.

Government Regulatory Activity

Another significant environmental force today is increasing government regulation. Even the current emphasis on reducing government involvement in the private sector does not obviate the long-term trend toward increasing government regulation. The idea of an open and free market system is recognized as more myth than reality.[24] As the regulator of last resort, government is forced to provide controls and standards. Pressures arise within organizations to circumvent or diminish such regulatory activity.

Hypothesis 25: Whistleblowing is more likely to occur when government regulatory activity increases.

Accountability of Government Officials

Citizens are becoming more concerned with the accountability of public agencies and government officials since "Watergate." The corruption of government officials was again brought to public consciousness with the "Abscam" convictions. As Vice-Presidents and Presidential candidates find their income tax returns very closely examined, greater scrutiny is brought to bear on the background and credibility of many other government officials.

Hypothesis 26: Whistleblowing is more likely to occur when greater accountability and higher standards are expected of government officials.

Professional Accountability

With the increasing professionalization of work and the demand for higher levels of education, professionals and other employees are expected to meet higher standards of performance and accountability in their work. Such pressures might be expected to lead to an increase in whistleblowing.

Hypothesis 27: Whistleblowing is more likely to occur when higher standards are imposed on professionals and other employees.

Ecological-Environmental and Health-Safety Problems

Public concern with ecological and environmental or health and safety problems is another force to be reckoned with. Business and government agencies must respond to new demands for the safe disposal of toxic wastes and the need to monitor carefully new industries and technologies such as nuclear plants gene splicing. They must also be more mindful of keeping their employees protected from dangerous work situations. This concern will inevitably require more expense for monitoring and developing new means of controlling such problems. These pressures can create fertile conditions for whistleblowing when there is a perceived failure to measure up to higher and more stringent standards.

Hypothesis 28: Whistleblowing is more likely to occur when there is increasing public concern for ecological and environmental or health and safety problems.

Media Focus on "White-Collar" Deviance

The media is one more force in the external environment of organizations that is having a powerful and increasing impact on whistleblowing. Reporters are becoming an effective and important means by which whistleblowers engage the attention of the public at large. Shocking and revealing headlines sell copy, and reporters are eager to uncover crime in the suites.[25] Certain types of individuals seek and enjoy the public spectacle that headlines provide.

Hypothesis 29: Whistleblowing is more likely to occur when the media attaches more importance to "white-collar" deviance.

Types of Environments

Emery and Trist classify four "ideal types" of environments according to the degree of "system connectedness" that exists among their components.[26] These ideal types are the placid, randomized environment; the placid, cluster environment; a disturbed-reactive environment; and a turbulent field.

The last has been hypothesized as the most relevant for understanding modern organizations. The turbulence results from the complexity and multiple character of the causal interconnections between the organization and its environment. Traditional organization structures and decision-making procedures are inadequate for effectively responding to such a turbulent environment. Inevitably conflicts arise and misperceptions occur. Organizations need to monitor this rapidly changing environment on a continuous basis. Their goals and policies will have to be continuously modified and innovative methods and policies developed to meet external challenges. If these modifications do not succeed, whistleblowing might occur as an adjustment through unofficial or external channels.

There are a number of problems in contemporary organizations that stand in the way of easy adjustments: (1) the environmental transactions cannot be explained by economic-rational criteria; (2) transactions involve whole system adaptation; and (3) transactions assume that a social responsibility exists. It will become increasingly important for organizations to surmount these obstacles to adapt to change.

Hypothesis 30: Whistleblowing is more likely when organizations do not effectively adapt to changes in their turbulent environments.

Because the organization is seen as not making necessary adaptations to the concerns raised, whistleblowers go outside of the organization to bring their complaints to individuals or groups whom they feel might bring pressure to bear. This can be seen as an attempt to make adaptations through an outside imposed mechanism. The whistleblower, however, is usually seen by the organization as a "deviant" who engages in damaging activity that warrants severe sanctions. A more appropriate response might be to examine the organizational system and seek improvements for effectively handling dissent within it.

Administrators and managers in established organizations, however, generally want the structure and procedures to remain as they are, for they know how to "do their thing" in the system, how to manipulate the power structure, and how to assure that their own needs and the needs of their unit are met. A more proactive approach is required if organizations are to adapt successfully. Whistleblowing might be expected to increase as long as rigidity and conformance to past practices prevail. Organizations must become increasingly aware of their responsibility for the social-economic-political impact of their functions. Top management will face increasing pressure to implement new structures and strategies to deal with shifting social values and concerns arising from the turbulent environment.

Hypothesis 30: Whistleblowing is more likely to occur when organizations rigidly conform to past practices rather than adopt new ones more suitable to their changed environments.

Inevitably it falls upon the shoulders of the people within the organization to respond to such concerns, for they affect the quality of their working life. Improving the internal processes can serve as a beginning for improving the effectiveness of transactions between organizations and their environments. A more enlightened approach to whistleblowing recognizes the need for such improvements.

This last section has focused on major environmental factors that related to whistleblowing. A number of hypotheses have been proposed. The major factors included the relationship between the organization and its environment, forces in the environment, and types of environment. The proposed hypotheses will have to be subjected to empirical verification.

CONCLUSION

Whistleblowing has been examined from three major theoretical perspectives: individual, organizational, and environmental. A number of theories and hypotheses within each of these areas has been explored for their potential help in the interpretation of this relatively new form of organizational behavior. The purpose of this chapter has been to provide a theoretical overview of the subject and to suggest new directions for a more detailed, and empirically based evaluation of the subject.

NOTES

1. For a discussion of the definitional problems see Chapter One of this volume.
2. There are other versions of the individual perspective, but these four appear to be the most promising for understanding whistleblowing.
3. Process interaction theory is elaborated in Albert K. Cohen, Deviance and Control (Englewood Cliffs, NJ: Prentice-Hall, 1966).
4. Herbert Blumer, Symbolic Interactionism: Perspectives and Method (Englewood Cliffs, NJ: Prentice-Hall, 1969).
5. See Edwin M. Schur, Labeling Deviant Behavior (New York: Harper and Row, 1971); also Erving Goffman, Stigma (Englewood Cliffs, NJ: Prentice-Hall, 1963).
6. Robert Presthus, The Organizational Society, revised edition (New York: St. Martin's Press, 1978).
7. See Hans H. Gerth and C. Wright Mills, Character and Social Structure (New York: Harcourt, Brace, and Co., 1953).
8. For an excellent discussion of this phenomenon, see Presthus, The Organizational Society.
9. See Robert M. Anderson, Robert Perrucci, Dan E. Schendel, and Leon Trachtman, Divided Loyalties: Whistleblowing at BART (West Lafayette, IN: Purdue University, 1980); also Richard W. Scott, "Professionals in Bureaucracies: Areas of Conflict," in Professionalization eds. H.M. Vollmer and D. Mills (Englewood Cliffs, NJ: Prentice-Hall, 1966).

10. An excellent discussion of reference group theory can be found in Robert K. Merton, Social Theory and Social Structure (New York: The Free Press, 1968).
11. Merton, Social Theory.
12. For a discussion of systems theory, see Fremont E. Kast and James E. Rosenweig, Contingency View of Organizations and Management (Chicago: Science Researchers Associates, 1973).
13. Rensis Likert, The Human Organization: Its Management and Value (New York: McGraw-Hill, 1967).
14. See James J. O'Toole, "Corporate and Managerial Cultures," in Behavioral Problems in Organizations ed. Gary L. Cooper (Englewood Cliffs, NJ: Prentice-Hall, 1979).
15. L.L. Barnard, The Field and Methods of Sociology (Norwood, PA: Norwood Editions, 1934).
16. Solomon E. Asch, Social Psychology (Englewood Cliffs, NJ: Prentice-Hall, 1952).
17. Richard Ritti, Engineer in the Industrial Corporation (New York: Columbia University Press, 1971).
18. Amitai Etzioni, "Social Control: Organizational Aspects," in The International Encyclopaedia of the Social Sciences (New York: The Free Press, 1968).
19. Jeffrey Pfeffer and Gerald Salancih, The External Control of Organizations (New York: Harper and Row, 1978).
20. Amitai Etzioni, A Comparative Analysis of Complex Organizations (New York: The Free Press, 1961).
21. Daniel Katz and Robert Kahn, The Social Psychology of Organizations (New York: John Wiley and Sons, 1966).
22. Stanley Young, Management: A Systems Analysis (Glenview, IL: Scott, Foresman and Co., 1976).
23. Alvin Toffler, The Third Wave (New York: Bantam Books, 1980) and John Naisbitt, Megatrends (New York: Warner, 1984).
24. Harry Magdoff and Paul M. Sweezy, The Deepening Crisis of U.S. Capitalism (New York: Monthly Review Press, 1981).
25. David R. Simon and D. Stanley Eitzen, Elite Deviance (Boston: Allyn and Bacon, 1982).
26. F.E. Emery and E.L. Trist, "The Causal Texture of Organizational Environments," Human Relations 18 (1965): 21-32.

THREE
THE CASE STUDY
METHOD AND ITS
APPLICATION

This chapter will discuss the use of the case study method. It is divided into two broad sections: the first provides a characterization of the case study method; the second describes the particular way in which we went about applying it in our project.

THE CASE STUDY METHOD

Selecting a Method

The case study method, in contrast to other research designs, was selected because it is best suited for an exploratory study such as ours where the scientific information or theoretical understanding is scant. When a research topic is in such an embryonic stage, it is appropriate to examine in depth and in detail a few representative cases in order to gain insights into the problem and generate hypotheses that can subsequently be tested by more quantitative approaches.[1] Sigmund Freud, for example, developed his remarkable insights into the human psyche through his examination and reflection upon his own dreams and the intensive study of his patients. We hope that our study of professional dissent can be similarly examined for insights into basic individual and organizational issues that can be pursued in more depth at a future date.

The case method has its parallels in two anthropological approaches to the study of human societies. The etic approach requires an objective, descriptive, and outside view of a culture. Anthropologists come equipped with their theories, hypotheses, and assumptions about the culture they are studying before they arrive. Their primary goal is to test them through direct observations. The emic approach emphasizes a completely different working methodology. The anthropologists suspend their theories, hypotheses, and assumptions and try to develop an awareness of the way the natives themselves interpret reality. It is an approach that tries to examine reality from the inside, from the perspective of the people themselves. The etic approach, on the other hand, tries to impose one's own views and models of the situation on the analysis.[2] The case study method adopts the emic approach.

The Nature of the Case Method

The basic methodological instrument utilized in this study is the case method. A case is

a story of organizational issues which actually have been faced by people, together with facts, opinions, and prejudices upon which decisions must be made. A key feature of a case is that decisions that require action must be made.[3]

It tries to portray the richness of the situation from the diverse perspectives of the individuals involved. This requires an alertness on the part of the investigators and a receptivity to differences in perception. The objects of study are allowed to guide the research process as new ideas, information, and insights emerge.

The case method allows for a much more intensive examination of a topic. Unlike quantitative studies, which seek to reduce a large number of phenomena to generalizable formulae, the case method focuses on relatively few situations and subjects them to intensive scrutiny. The goal is a clearer, richer, and more accurate depiction of social reality as experienced by the protagonists, rather than as it is reconstructed by the social scientists.[4]

This approach requires researchers to rely on their integrative powers to draw together many bits of information into a coherent whole. They must hold in check their own speculations and exercise caution in selecting what they believe to be important.

Its Limitations

The case method has its limitations. First, two cases comparable in all essential respects can rarely be found. In another organization of another size, the same factors may result in a different outcome, or a similar outcome handled in a different way. Extrapolation from the cases we have examined is always tenuous. The method is suggestive but not conclusive.

Second, the case studies can seldom be repeated exactly or their findings fully verified. They involve a unique assemblage of factors occurring at a specific point in time.

Third, the significance of the findings is left to the interpretation of the researchers. They assemble the case out of a variety of facts and portray events based on their own training, interests, and preconceptions, which may inadvertently distort it. For example, a philosopher who believes the world is rational and ordered may describe the same events in a much different way from a sociologist focused on contingencies. In this study the research team included representatives of these and other disciplines in order to mitigate this orientation and its biases.

Finally, the results of a case study are based on a small sample, and the ability to generalize from them is limited.[5] The presentation of a variety of cases in this study has helped to mitigate this limitation.

Its Use

Our study examined several cases involving professional dissent. An attempt has been made to study each from a variety of different perspectives-- individual, organizational, strategic, and moral. The major actors have been allowed to speak for themselves, and information has been presented concerning the features, characteristics, and workings of the organizations involved. In some instances additional information has been supplied that provides a more accurate understanding of relevant factors involved in the case. In all circumstances the attempt has been made to portray the situation as it unfolded and to allow the reader to become immersed in the flow of events as they occurred and to draw his or her own conclusions.

A major goal of our study was to understand the factors that lead to disagreements in the workplace and the range of strategies available to resolve them. In so doing we sought to capture the tensions and dynamics of professional dissent as an important and timely issue for all employees and employers. Our analyses are directed to students and faculty in schools of business in the hope that the hypotheses and theories generated would serve as guides to future studies and research and assist them in understanding the nature and roots of corporate power.[6]

SELECTING THE CASES

The Literature Search

As a first step to identifying actual cases for investigation, we undertook an extensive literature search. It took several forms: first, an examination of theoretical writings on organizations and professional ethics; second, a hand search of magazines and newspaper articles, and key publications such as the Federal Times; and third, a computer-assisted search of relevant data bases in the humanities, social sciences, business, and government. A list of the data bases used, as well as the number of citations provided by each, is contained in Appendix One. After reviewing the initial printouts, additional leads were investigated, and specific cases were targeted for further research.

On the whole these computer searches were helpful, but incomplete and problematic. They tended to require a focus that was either too broad or too narrow. If we restricted these searches to only items that used the expression "whistleblowing" and its cognates "blowing the whistle," "whistleblowers" and "blow the whistle," we failed to identify relevant materials about instances of whistleblowing, but not so called. Ironically, we also encountered the opposite problem. Much that was irrelevant for our purposes was included under this rubric: despite our best efforts, we could not exclude several references to the old song "Hear That Lonesome Whistle Blow"!

Some examples of the latter problem seem humorous and innocuous but posed difficult conceptual problems. In the popular literature the expression "whistleblowing" is very general, ranging over different practices that bear a "family resemblance" to each other, but that do not fit a single definition. Accordingly, one of our first conceptual tasks was to refine the notion of whistleblowing so that we were focused on a unitary phenomenon and were not studying several different events.

Targeting the Phenomenon

In the course of formulating a definition of whistleblowing, we decided to exclude many instances that others called whistleblowing. Chapter One, as well as the first portion of Chapter Ten,[7] addressed this and other conceptual issues in defining the subject matter of our inquiry. Whistleblowing occurs when each of the following four conditions is satisfied: 1) an individual performs an act intended to make information public; 2) the information becomes a matter of public record; 3) the information is about possible or actual, nontrivial wrongdoing in an organization; and 4) the individual who performs the action is a member or former member of the organization in which the wrongdoing or possible wrongdoing takes place.

Our initial scheme for categorizing cases involved three variables: whistleblowing versus nonwhistleblowing; successful versus unsuccessful; and public versus private. These yielded a total of eight categories into which a case could fall. Dr. Deborah Johnson's paper, which formed the core of Chapter One, was useful in articulating the criteria for drawing the first distinction. Our project also had to come to grips with a second question: How does one decide when an individual's action is successful? Here again we found the popular discussions less precise than scientific research would allow. Some individuals were too modest, taking insufficient credit for the results of their actions. Others were too ambitious, claiming for themselves the achievements of others. We realized as well that an individual's actions are only one factor in affecting the conduct of corporations, and are very difficult to weigh in comparison with the actions of others and a host of other factors—such as changes in technology, decisions and recommendations of regulatory agencies, or broad economic trends. We had to draw a line along a continuum of change: How much of a difference, and of what sort, must an individual's actions have before we categorize them as successful? A related question is: What makes one strategy more likely to succeed than its alternatives? This question is partially answered in terms of appropriateness. Congress may be an effective mechanism for raising some issues while inappropriate for others. The courts redress personal wrongdoing, but do not always respond to the dissident's other concern, namely organizational wrongdoing. Chapters One and Eight discuss the criteria for each strategy's success, and address this question of appropriateness.

In a second working paper by Dr. Johnson, five criteria for success were articulated.[8] Any one will be sufficient for calling an individual's act of dissent successful: 1) the whistleblower's concerns are shown to be unfounded; 2) there is a policy change; 3) the wrongdoing stops; 4) the organization is prosecuted and convicted; or 5) individuals are able to avoid being victims of the wrongdoing. In the course of our research, we extended Dr. Johnson's definitions of success to all dissidents within an organization, not just those who go outside the organization and are therefore termed "whistleblowers" in her limited sense. We defined a nonwhistleblower as someone who fell within the following two categories: a dissident who tries to work within the organization to effect change; or someone who has an ethical or moral obligation to dissent, but for various reasons chose not to do so.

Additional Strategies

In conjunction with the newspaper searches, several different approaches were used to identify both whistleblowing and nonwhistleblowing cases. One such approach focused on cases in which individuals were unjustly discharged. Media coverage of the dismissals or publicity arising out of the court cases attracted our attention.

A related approach focused on cases in which there was an investigation into the seriousness of the harm done. For example, in 1975 Dr. Chou, an independent physician, made the connection between his patients' symptoms and kepone poisoning. An investigation was subsequently initiated and publicized through the newspapers.

Business and government journals also provided several possible cases. Business and Society Review, which publishes a quarterly review of notable company achievements and failures in areas of public concern, proved to be very informative.

One final approach involved personal contact with scholars such as Alan Westin and David Ewing, both of whom are familiar with the areas of professional dissent and employee rights. We found it helpful to contact organizations such as the Institute for Policy Studies (IPS) in Washington, which includes the Government Accountability Project (GAP). Mr. Thomas Devine and Mr. Louis Clark of that office made helpful suggestions on more than one occasion about individuals and organizations.

Final Case Selection

At the outset 27 cases were tentatively considered. An organization was selected on the basis of one of the following criteria: 1) the organization had experienced a whistleblowing incident; 2) it had faced a controversial situation characterized by a professional difference of opinion, but one in which no whistleblowing had occurred; or 3) the organization had been identified for its leadership in finding alternatives for dealing effectively with professional dissent. In addition to the above guidelines, case selection was confined to those involving scientists and engineers in high technology organizations.

Several cases were eliminated because they were too old. Given this fact, the probability of informant recall would have been too low to warrant studying the case. In other cases key informants could not be located. Finally, one additional criterion entered into the selection process --the strategy employed by the dissident. In each case we wanted to highlight a different way of voicing professional dissent. Several of the remaining cases represented duplicate strategies and therefore were excluded. Altogether seven cases were targeted for the research project.

NOTES

1. Claire Selltiz, Lawrence S. Wrightsman, and Stuart W. Cook, Research Methods in Social Relations, 3rd. ed. (New York: Holt, Rinehart and Winston, 1976), pp. 96-99.
2. K.L. Pike, Language in Relation to a Unified Theory of the Structure of Human Behavior, parts 1-3 (Paris: Mouton and Cie Editions, 1967).
3. Kenneth L. Bernhardt and Thomas C. Kinnear, Cases in Marketing Management (Dallas: Business Publications, Inc., 1978), p. 3.
4. Peter Berger and Thomas Luckmann, The Social Construction of Reality (New York: Doubleday and Company, 1966).
5. Based in part on Robert J. House, "Scientific Investigation in Management," Management International Review (1970): pp. 141-142.
6. See Chapter One (this volume).
7. See pages 3-13 (this volume); and Frederick A. Elliston, "Anonymous Whistleblowing," Business and Professional Ethics 1 (Winter 1982): 39-59; and Chapter Ten (this volume).
8. Deborah Johnson, "Successful Whistle Blowing," Unpublished Paper, Rensselaer Polytechnic Institute, Troy, New York, 1981; and Chapter One (this volume).

APPENDIX: DATA BASES SEARCHED BY COMPUTER
AND THE RESULTS

Data Base	Number of Citations
Abstracts in Psychology (PSYC)	1
Books Information	11

(INFO)

Educational Research Information Center (ERIC)	0
Index Medicus (MESH)	0
Magazine Index	7
Legal Research	0
Management Contents (MGMT)	13
Medical Libraries (MEDLARS)	0
National Clearinghouse for Mental Health Information (NCMHI)	2
National Technology Information Service (NTIS)	0
New York Times Index (NYTS)	10
Public Affairs Information Service (PAIS)	0
Science Search (SCISEARCH)	10
Smithsonian (SMITH)	0
Social Science Citation Index (SSCI)	15
TOTAL	74

PART TWO
EXECUTING THE RESEARCH DESIGN

FOUR
INTERVIEWING
INFORMANTS

This chapter will examine the way in which we gathered our information. The first section describes the interview schedule, informant selection, and procedures for arranging the interviews. The second outlines various techniques utilized in the interviewing stage: the use of open-ended questions, single versus tandem interviewing, the use of the tape recorder, and telephone versus on-site interviewing. A brief discussion of the importance of gathering additional data is also included.

PREPARING FOR THE INTERVIEW

The Design of the Interview Schedule

Unlike most previous research on professional dissent, our study was theoretically guided, comparative, and employed a field research methodology. Our original grant proposal suggested a dual frame of reference--that is, we were to be both philosophical and behavioral in our approach. In the first phase, which involved the conceptualization of whistle-blowing and the selection of cases, we employed both approaches. The philosophical perspective came into play in analyzing the concept of whistleblowing, which in turn facilitated our case selection; the sociological perspective informed the interview schedule. Both of these perspectives

were used in the later phase of the project: cases were analyzed to test the hypotheses embedded in the interview
schedule and suggested by organizational theory; and an ethical analysis identified moral issues in each case and appraised the conflicting principles on which they were based.
This dual strategy was adopted for several reasons: the existing literature on whistleblowing was significantly lack-
ing in systematic and theoretically grounded descriptions;
and the basic concept of whistleblowing was vague with unclear boundaries and ambiguous moral overtones.

We were then confronted with the problem of choosing
among behavioral theories. Any one of several could have
been employed. A psychological theory could have guided our
research toward individual differences between whistleblowers and non-whistleblowers; or a socio-psychological
framework could have sensitized our study to the potential
ego-environment interaction that gives rise to or impedes
assumption of a whistleblowing role. A sociological theory
could have addressed intra- and inter-role conflict in organizations, as was suggested in the preceding chapter. We decided to retain the organization as our primary focus, while
still using the other theoretical perspectives to inform our
accounts. There are several reasons for this emphasis on the
organization.

The empirical literature on whistleblowing has pointed
to the organization rather than to the individual as the
most important unit of analysis. Perrucci et al.[1],
Waters[2], and Perrucci[3] have decided that in order to
understand the phenomenon of whistleblowing, one must examine organizational rather than personal behavior. Therefore,
our cases are not primarily concerned with persons who have
blown the whistle or events of whistleblowing in the organization, but with organizations that experienced (or avoided)
whistleblowing in the course of organizational politics.
More precisely, it was the strategy available to organizational members that was critical for our purposes in understanding why someone blows the whistle and what accounts for
his or her success or failure.

This decision offered a number of advantages. First, by
focusing on the organizational context, we were able to
raise significant questions and generate at least partial answers about the relationship of the organization to its environment. Second, we were able to examine the impact of varying technology on the likelihood of the occurrence of
whistleblowing. Third, we were able to address the question
of whether some organizations are more responsible than
others, either in the way they conceive relevant constituencies or in the way they choose to pursue the variety of technical and ethical alternatives raised by their own staff.

Fourth, we were able to provide answers--albeit only tentatively--about the probability of whistleblowing occurring in some organizations rather than others, and whether its use is more likely to produce organizational change in some forms of organizations than others. Fifth, because our locus of study was the organization, the ethical and policy considerations deal with organizational, rather than personal, behavior. Thus, the implications of this study are relevant to broad questions about the control of organizations. Sixth, according to our operational definition of whistleblowing, whistleblowers seek change in organizations and seek to guide organizational behavior. Our empirical effort is designed to examine organizational guidance processes and the mechanisms for dealing with the dissent and dissension that would otherwise disrupt them.

In contrast there are opportunity costs. First, by focusing on organizations rather than on persons, we stand to lose some, but not all, of the information relevant to the personal choices of people who decide to dissent publicly from the decisions of their peers. Second, we lose some, but not all, of the information concerning the personal difficulties that may follow such action. Third, we lose, to a lesser extent, the ability to study the immediate work group or similar environments that intervene between the person and the organization.

Because of the constraints of time, resources and access to organizations, we were unable to undertake complete surveys of organizational participant behaviors and attitudes. We chose to rely instead on organizational informants and to bolster their accounts with a variety of other data sources, for example, documents, newspaper articles, and annual reports. In order to make comparisons across organizations, our contacts with the informants selected had to be relatively uniform. To ensure uniformity, we sought to obtain information relevant to the identical dimension from each person. The content of the interview schedule was governed by the selection of these dimensions.

Informant Selection

The rationale for interviewing the dissident in a study of professional dissent is obvious and needs no justification. Whether an individual decides to blow the whistle on questionable deeds of his or her employer is, in the final analysis, that individual's personal choice. It is necessary to appreciate his or her perspective on this and other aspects of his or her job in order to understand the decisions made by someone faced with this dilemma. An interview with the whistleblower or non-whistleblower is essential. It is the most direct way of assessing his or her organization's policy decisions and the impact of the organization's action.

However, the basic reasons underlying the decision to interview other people in the organization might not appear so obvious. The decision to identify and interview people who occupied strategic organizational positions at the time period in which the controversial events unfolded was based on two considerations.

First, people in key roles are rich sources of important information for accurately gauging the organization's response to internal dissent. The mechanisms and processes employed by the organization to resolve internal disputes provide insight into the organization and could reveal a relationship between these methods and the actions taken by the dissidents and non-dissidents. Such data are fundamental to the development of testable hypotheses regarding the conditions that contribute to the escalation of professional objection to whistleblowing.

Second, to understand whistleblowing one needs to understand the environment in which it occurs. To appreciate the judgments of the individuals involved, one must delineate the social system in which those judgments are made. Premature or incomplete conclusions regarding individual decisions become more likely the further one separates those decisions from their social context. For the purposes of this study, the organization is a primary social system that must be considered when analyzing data on corporate and professional decisions.

Initial interviewing decisions were based on factors that would provide an understanding of the social system, the professional's decisions, and the organization's actions. There were three theoretical perspectives which were appropriate for achieving these objectives: organizational control, organizational roles, and the organizational environment. Each of these is composed of several variables.

Given the assumption that the organization's control systems are important sources of data, as suggested in Chapter Two, it becomes necessary to identify the components of the control networks. These include the personnel division, the budget office, legal affairs, quality control, and the Management Information System (MIS). Many of these divisions (or their equivalents) can be found in all organizations. Although their forms will vary, the five divisions represent functions that are vital to the operation of any agency. The organization's efforts to avoid internal dissent, resolve the disagreement, or react to it should be seen in the actions of some, or all, of these divisions.

This emphasis on control networks does not imply, of course, that others should not be interviewed. One must remember the important role played by the executive officers in this scheme. Senior management often sets the tone of the organization and provides overall direction through the control network. Organizations will vary in the methods used and the objectives sought, but each organization will make value decisions within its control system.

Interviewing individuals who hold the six types of positions outlined previously also serves purposes beyond analyzing the control variables. The control systems' regulations, procedures, and sanctions comprise an important element of the organization's social environment. As mentioned earlier, this is the context in which a dissident's decisions and behavior take place. The relevance to a study of professional dissent and whistleblowing seems clear. Furthermore, and perhaps more importantly, the data gathered from interviewing these key people might provide insight into questions that are difficult, if not impossible, to answer. One example is that of goals. Whether one is concerned with organizational or individual goals, they are notoriously difficult to isolate and specify, but if we assume that behavior is purposive, then we might begin to develop a picture of an organization's goals by studying the actions and decisions of those key individuals.

Many of these key positions involve roles and responsibilities beyond their control functions. All organizations are involved in interactions with the external environment. These relationships are outside the narrowly defined boundaries of an agency, but are important factors in its behavior: no organization is an island. Numerous reciprocal exchanges take place between individuals in the external environment and organizational representatives. People holding privileged positions in the hierarchy, as well as a few lower-level persons, are repeatedly involved in such boundary-spanning activities. Although there is a variety of perspectives regarding the precise nature of the relationship between an organization and its environment, it is clear that these interactions cannot be ignored.

One way to investigate this network is from "inside" the host organization. This allows the researchers to gain insight into the way in which relationships with a specified environment influence the internal decisions of an organization.

A different view of these relationships and the way in which they affect decisions can be acquired from a vantage point outside the organization. To do so we needed to identify the agents within a specified environment. Interviews were conducted with informants from external organizations which interacted with members of the host organization on a regular basis, or at critical junctures in incidents discussed.

Arranging the Interviews

The dissident or non-dissident was contacted initially to request his or her consent to be interviewed. This first contact also afforded our staff an opportunity to request missing names of role incumbents or additional facts concerning the incident.

We sought permission to interview inside the selected organization by first contacting the chief executive officer. In some cases final permission was granted by an administrative assistant or a deputy commissioner. In others no such permission from the organization was required, but each member seemed to be authorized to decide for himself or herself. Both telephone calls and individual letters were employed to enlist cooperation in this process. During the early stages of the project, the latter procedure was primarily utilized. We believed that a formal request in writing would secure greater cooperation. However, we found this was not always the case. Comparing the two methods, we found that initial telephone calls requesting participation in the study was the more productive alternative. Only two refusals resulted out of 37 telephoned requests, whereas seven refusals resulted out of 12 written requests, six of which did not bother to respond.

In requesting the appointments, we discussed the increased attention now being given to social responsibility of large organizations and the obligations of professional scientists or engineers toward their employers, their profession, and the public. We mentioned that the results of our study would have important consequences for companies faced with professional dissent and that information on the causes and nature of professional disagreements would influence organizational design and agency management and benefit professionals employed in these organizations. The study's sponsor was also mentioned, along with the necessity and importance of the interviews. The time between initial contact and the actual interview varied from a few days to several weeks.

All informants were asked to sign a consent form at the outset of the interview. The original consent form offered the following three options in regard to confidentiality: 1) I am willing to be identified by name; 2) I wish to be identified only by role in an unnamed organization; or 3) I wish to be identified only by role in a named organization.

A few persons expressed a desire to select the appropriate option at the close of the interview. Other than this preference to postpone choosing an option, no significant problems for those interviewed were associated with the consent form.

At the second yearly review by the Institutional Review Board at the Michael J. Hindelang Criminal Justice Research Center, in accordance with the requirements of the Department of Health and Human Services regulation concerning Protection of Human Subjects (45CFR46), it was determined that the information disclosed by the informants and subsequently reported could lead to reprisals against the informant or third-party human subjects named in the interview. The board determined to its satisfaction that the following safeguard against the specified risk was to be taken. The above three options were to be deleted from the consent form and replaced with "information that could lead to identification will be deleted from the transcripts of the interview and from all written and oral communications of the project. Every effort will be made to ensure that actual persons and organizations participating in this research project will not be identified, either directly or by implication."

This meant that those persons who had already signed consent forms had to be contacted again for the purpose of securing their signatures on the revised form. Any future informants would be asked to sign the new form.

INTERVIEWING TECHNIQUES

The Use of Open-Ended Questions

In designing an interview schedule, a researcher must decide between two question formats: open-ended or free responses, which permit the informants to answer in their own words; or closed-ended or fixed responses, which require that informants choose their answers from a predetermined list. For several reasons we opted for the former.

First, the phrasing of open-ended questions is closer to ordinary conversation, thereby helping to sustain an easy rapport. We wanted our informants to feel that they were engaged in casual conversation with a colleague. Open-ended questions help achieve this feeling.

Second, open-ended questions are more effective in revealing the informants' own definition of the situation. Because they are not provided with a list of possible answers from which to choose, informants are free to respond within their own frame of reference This latitude is especially important in a study such as ours where the issues are complex and some relevant dimensions are unknown.

Third, if an informant does not understand the question correctly, the misunderstanding will more likely be evident in his or her answer. The question can immediately be rephrased so as to elicit an appropriate response. A closed-ended question that has been misunderstood is not as readily detected.

Fourth, open-ended questions were the more suitable alternative for use with our interviewing technique, which we shall call the "focused-elite." It is a combination of Merton and Kendall's[4] focused interview and Dexter's[5] elite interview.

In a focused interview, the interviewer describes a particular experience and its effects. All persons whom we interviewed were believed to have been involved in the situation in one way or another. They were asked about their experiences in an effort to ascertain their personal definition of the situation. This strategy is amenable to hypothesis testing because the interview schedule sets forth the major areas of inquiry, with the hypotheses built into the framework of topics to be covered. The ordering of the questions, as well as their elaboration and emphasis, are left to the interviewer's discretion because he or she is in control of the interview. Questions serve only as guides. The interviewer has the freedom to pursue unanticipated responses and to explore reasons and motives for actions taken, but must limit the informant to a discussion of the relevant issues.

Elite interviewing, on the other hand, involves an informant who is given special, non-standardized treatment. Many of our informants were high-ranking government officials and business executives who would not be receptive to the more usual question-and-answer style of interviewing. In these instances we once again stressed their definitions of the situation, but allowed them wide latitude to introduce what they regarded as relevant. The informant was given the opportunity to construct his or her own account of the situation and events.

One drawback of this method, however, is that informants' thoughts often go into tangential areas. As a result, the interview may be time-consuming with few productive results. The interviewers learned early in the project to gently guide the conversation, thereby keeping the discussion within the desired parameters. A related drawback, and a disadvantage to the use of open-ended questions in general, is that of unfulfilled objectives. Occasionally, we found that informants responded in a general, rather than a specific, fashion. Broad answers to specific questions are not satisfactory. Evasion also occurs when the informant interprets the question differently from the interviewer. For example, a subordinate who has been asked how he or she thinks his or her new manager will compare with the previous one may only utter statements that he or she hopes will be democratic, without really making any comparisons to the former superior. To compensate for this, probes or follow-up questions had to be employed.

Varying frames of reference are another source of difficulty associated with the use of open-ended questions. Often one may view a question from different perspectives. In this regard a special effort was made to not only identify personal motivation for individual behavior, but to elicit an explanation of events observed only by the informant. Therefore, unless open-ended questions were designed to consider all possible underlying reasons for behavior, both his or her own and others', the informant might have omitted relevant data. Alternatively, if a single frame of reference was desired, along with a corresponding level of explanation, the language of the question(s) had to be phrased so that answers based on alternative frames of reference would be excluded.

One final disadvantage to free-response questioning relates to the analysis of the data gathered in this way. Since the ultimate purpose of most research is to draw comparisons among individuals, or in this case organizations, the wide disparity in answers should be reduced to one set of categories that will permit comparisons. Once these common categories are designed, into which all answers can be classified, the effort of analyzing and comparing the interviews begins. No coding, however, was used in this project, due mainly to budget restrictions and the small sample. Comparisons among organizations were handled in a substantive manner by using excerpts from transcripts, much like those employed by Hans Toch in his analyses.[6]

In terms of data analysis, we were interested in identifying the organizations most likely to experience a whistleblowing event and where in the organization this event would occur. A number of hypotheses were generated (see Chapter Two and Appendix One) and tested on the data. Our research also focused on strategies for resolving differences. For example, which strategy is the most appropriate choice in a given situation? Is that particular strategy successful in resolving the whistleblower's concerns? Chapter Eight, A Strategic Analysis, discusses the appropriateness of each strategy in terms of several factors: professional roles, individual characteristics, organizational structure, the issue, and the historical context. Moreover, the authors appraise each strategy in terms of its own measure of success.

Single Versus Tandem Interviewing

At the beginning of the interviewing phase, most of the interviews were conducted by two research associates, George Capowich and Paula Lockhart, both of whom had been involved in the project since the early exploratory stages. All early interviews were conducted in the offices of the informants and ranged from one to one-and-one-half hours.

The man-woman team or tandem interviewing method served as an alternative to the more standard single-interviewer technique. The strategy afforded numerous advantages. First, the interviewers obtained more information in a shorter period of time. Because we only had one interview with a given informant and had originally been allotted one hour in which to conduct the interview, it was necessary to compile as much information as possible, thereby reducing the follow-up work. Second, this procedure resulted in a much smoother and cogent discussion. Each informant was made to feel as though he or she were a colleague and that we regarded this study as a joint effort. The usual interviewer-informant type of atmosphere was thus avoided. Both interviewers were able to devote full attention to the informants. Informants were able to talk freely at their normal pace without interruptions. Third, if one interviewer missed the significance of a comment, the other interviewer usually detected it and probed for more details. Fourth, with two interviewers it was possible to take full advantage of the informant's knowledge and expertise. Most were very articulate individuals, capable of responding to questions rather quickly. A single interviewer might have had a more difficult time eliciting information. Fifth, it is possible that an informant might have reacted negatively to an interviewer. If this situation had occurred, a second interviewer would most likely have been able to salvage the interview. Experience has shown that it is unlikely that an informant will react negatively to both interviewers.

In written or memory-reconstructed interviews, there is an unconscious or conscious bias on the part of the interviewer concerning which information to write down. This selective recording was eliminated by tape-recording the entire conversation. This meant first that we had an accurate record of each interview, to which we could return later for answers to questions that arose.

Second, we had a more complete record, which was less prone to errors of omissions due to lapses of attention.

Third, by using the tape recorder we were able to complete more interviews within a specified period of time. We found the maximum number to be three interviews for each day. The time and labor involved in writing or reconstructing interviews was thereby significantly reduced.

Fourth, the interviewer can immediately record his or her comments directly on tape after the interview. Often it is not possible to write out one's impressions.

Fifth, the interviewer, free from note taking, is able to devote his or her full attention to the informant. Conversation occurs at a normal pace.

Although economical in terms of the interviewer's time and labor, consideration was given to the supplementary expenditure of money involved in using the tape recorder. The costs associated with transcription were a large expense. The cost averaged approximately $1.25 for each page for a draft, which was then checked for accuracy, edited for fluency, and corrected for typographical errors--probably bringing the total to $5.00 for each page or $100 for each transcript.

Several concerns or questions are frequently raised in social research concerning the effect of the tape recorder. One question is: Will the use of the tape recorder result in a higher refusal rate? Based on our experience and that of other researchers, the answer is "No." The introduction of the tape recorder resulted in only one refusal out of all the interviews conducted.

A second question often asked is: Will the use of the tape recorder diminish interviewer-informant rapport? For reasons mentioned earlier, our experience also suggests a negative answer to this question. The interviewer(s), free from note taking, were able to give their full attention to the informant, thereby increasing rapport. Conversation occurred at a normal pace without the disruptive aspect associated with a written interview. It is noteworthy that several persons with whom we spoke tended to lower their voices when confidential incidents were being discussed. The tape recorder picked up this difference in tone that otherwise would have been unrecorded. One informant asked to have the recorder turned off at one point during the conversation, whereas others stated that their comments were off the record.

There are several practical problems connected with the use of the tape recorder that should be discussed. First, a tape recorder often picks up a lot of outside noise--air conditioners, doors being shut, and the shuffling of papers. Several of our tapes were inaudible in places due to the noise level. This is usually not a problem in telephone recording. Second, there is a possibility of mechanical failure. While one researcher was interviewing several hundred miles from the office, the tape recorder began to sporadically speed up and slow down while taping. Rewinding and checking the first few moments of conversation, which was standard procedure, did not catch the problem. It became apparent during transcription, too late to correct it. As a result, one interview was lost. Third, careless practices on the part of the interviewer can result in a waste of project funds since interviews then have to be repeated. There are several practices that should be mentioned. Failure to take extra tapes to the interview is one, forgetting to install new batteries or to check the old ones is another. An electrical outlet may not be available. One half of an entire interview did not record when the interviewer did not depress the record button firmly enough. One other pragmatic concern relates to turning the cassette tape over at the end of side one. It is very easy, once the interview begins, to forget about the tape. Valuable pieces of information could be lost as a consequence. Although the interviewer should not stare at the machine, he or she should learn to gauge the time for each side.

Telephone Versus On-Site Interviewing

Strict adherence to the budget did not permit the additional expenditure of traveling to a distant city in which only one or two interviews were to be conducted. Rather than lose valuable pieces of information, taped telephone interviews were used as a substitute.

The use of telephone interviews is quite common in marketing research, public opinion polls, and survey research.[7] In recent years the technique has been effectively used in social research. For example, this approach was used exclusively by Anderson and Perrucci in their well-received study on BART.[8] As a method of gathering data, it offers a number of advantages over traditional approaches.

First, considering the travel time and cost involved in a face-to-face interview, telephone interviewing is less expensive. Any question that can be asked in person can be posed over the telephone, except questions that require visual cues.

Second, related to this cost reduction is a parallel savings in interviewer time. Interviews were completed more economically with no discernible decrease in quality. Our telephone interviews averaged 30 to 45 minutes, compared to one hour to an hour-and-a-half for face-to-face interviews.

Third, informants seemed to be less distracted by out-side interference when talking on the telephone than when speaking in person. The result was not just more economical but more concentrated, intense, and coherent.

Fourth, the interviewer could obtain answers to follow-up questions quickly by using this method. Telephone calls can be made quickly and important additional information readily obtained.

Fifth, bias resulting from the effect of the interviewer on the informant is reduced. Mannerisms, style of dress, race, and all other characteristics, except voice and sex, are masked.

Sixth, a telephone call helps ensure confidentiality. It is a private conversation, usually not overheard by out-siders. It if is overheard, the outsider is privy to only one side. A few informants, who would not agree to speak in person for fear of retaliation or embarrassment, did agree to telephone interviews. Without this approach, important da-ta would have been lost.

Telephone interviewing is easy to conduct. One can be more objective because there are no visual cues to which to respond. Taping the conversation is accomplished by using a cassette recorder and an inexpensive telephone recorder jack, which is sold at any local stereo store.

As with any method, there are several problems with using the telephone interview technique. Complicated ques-tions and length of interview may rule it out as a strategy for collecting information. Since a lot of informants are quite busy, an interviewer will usually get only one inter-view. Other disadvantages are evident, however.

First, there is a loss of visual cues--gestures and facial expressions. Oftentimes, what one says conflicts with how one is acting at the time it is said. We attempted to counteract this loss by employing a tape recorder. Subtle nuances and inflections in the voice served adequately as an alternative indicator.

Second, rapport is not easily established and main-tained when there is no face-to-face exchange. Realizing this drawback, we attempted to speak with the informants at least once, probably twice, before conducting the interview. The initial call was devoted to explaining the project and to scheduling a future appointment. A personal follow-up letter was then sent reiterating what had been said, along with the consent form. In the course of this initial call, the prospective informant was allowed to discuss other mat-ters and encouraged to ask questions regarding our project staff. The actual interview was conducted during the second or third call, after the formalities had been addressed and rapport established.

Third, valuable bits and pieces of information that would be obtained before or after the interview are lost. Although the interview may be formally over, informants are likely to continue the discussion while walking down the hallway or while the interviewer is getting ready to leave. For example, one informant related a significant piece of information to the interviewer while they were driving to the airport. He had not discussed it during the interview. The interviewer also learns something about a person by experiencing his or her "world"--the arrangement and contents of his or her office, memorabilia, and personal effects. The interviewer also gains an insight from an informant's physical demeanor, body language, and composure.

Fourth, in the past, researchers have suggested that people seem to express their attitudes and opinions in more detail when contacted in person than when interviewed over the telephone.[9] Comparing the average length of responses to specified questions asked of informants in face-to-face interviews (73 percent) and telephone interviews (27 percent), we found a slight but not significant difference in responses. The average length of a telephone transcript was 16 single-spaced pages, while the average for face-to-face was 18 single-spaced pages.

This finding is consistent with more recent studies. Joseph Hochstim found in his study of three information gathering strategies that by using the telephone to acquire the desired data, the quality of the interview may actually be increased: the interviewers are more at ease working from familiar surroundings and the informants are more candid than they would be in a face-to-face interview.[10]

The utility of telephone interviewing was also demonstrated in a study of New York State physicians conducted by the National Opinion Research Center (NORC).[11] Unlike our study, their telephone interviews were longer--averaging an hour and a half. A small subsample of the cases (20 percent) were interviewed in person to facilitate comparisons. Negligible response differences were found between telephone and face-to-face methods. Telephone interviews seemed to elicit responses less distorted in the direction of social acceptability than responses obtained face-to-face.

Gathering Additional Data

Only one other whistleblowing study has made a deliberate attempt to bring additional perspectives to bear on a whistleblowing event. In **Divided Loyalties**, Perrucci et al. interviewed the BART engineers, management, the directors, and members of the California Society of Professional

Engineers (CSPE) and the National Society of Professional Engineers (NSPE) in order to present their independent viewpoints.[12] Each author examined and represented the viewpoints of only one of the groups. Aside from telephone interviews with the principal actors, they relied on the performance evaluations of the three engineers; minutes from professional society meetings; internal memoranda; letters to and from CSPE and NSPE; newspaper accounts; and a report prepared by a legislative analyst.

The remaining studies, Nader,[13] Westin,[14] and Mitchell,[15] have been less ambitious. For example, Nader's accounts are a result of a 1971 conference on whistleblowing, while four of Westin's ten accounts originate from a panel on "Whistle Blowing, Loyalty and Dissent in Corporate Life" held in 1978. Mitchell's recent book depends largely on the accounts of individual whistleblowers.

By contrast, we requested and examined almost 1,000 pages of memoranda, letters, reports, and investigative summaries. Significantly, however, this request took over six months to process, and the Inspector General previously in charge was willing to make a (small) wager we would receive nothing. After hearing one informant's story of why he was demoted, our staff hand-searched the governor's campaign records. Although no firm connection between his demotion and the governor's office could be made, the search did reveal a questionable campaign contribution from the head of a large petroleum company to the re-election committee for the governor of the state.

Overall, the supporting information was relatively easy to acquire. Simply by telephoning the organization one can obtain copies of annual reports. They were all received within a few weeks of the initial call. A university library or government depository has all the congressional hearing reports, while citations for newspaper articles, books, and professional journal articles are readily retrieved through a computer-assisted search. For a modest price, the legal briefs were obtained directly from the attorneys involved. The court opinions, on the other hand, were located in court reporters found on the shelves of any university or law library.

Aside from the external interviews, the data of greatest assistance were the legal briefs, court opinions, and the Freedom of Information request materials. The newspaper articles and congressional hearing reports were useful for background information only. Annual reports were of little assistance since they contained mainly financial information.

Compared to the interviews with organizational informants, the supporting evidence was worthwhile for several reasons.

First, it increased the accuracy of our data. Several of our cases were more than five years old and the informants occasionally had a hard time remembering correct dates, names, and specific occurrences. Additional data on the case served as corroboration.

Second, the supporting data were of assistance in filling the gaps. Oftentimes we were unable to interview everyone who played a part in the event under study. From documented reports, memoranda, letters, and accounts, we were able to discern the role played by these missing informants. Moreover, a few informants did not tell us the whole story, either intentionally or by mistake. But we were able to compensate because we had the information on record elsewhere.

Third, our interviews were made shorter and more to the point as a result of additional data. It was not necessary to discuss events in depth because we had previously acquired the details. Once we had verified with the informant that the statements attributed to them were correct, or that the document was a fair indication of what had transpired, we were free to pursue other areas.

Fourth, informants were more receptive to the interviewer if she had done her homework. In fact, one informant refused to speak with the interviewer until documents she regarded as relevant were reviewed by the project staff. Finally, if the interviewer is knowledgeable about the case, conversation can occur at a normal pace without the assistance of notes. Rapport is enhanced.

CONCLUSION

This chapter has explored the various techniques and methodologies employed in a research project on professional dissent. Beginning with a literature search, which encompassed hand searching magazines and newspapers and computer-assisted searches, which reviewed periodicals and other data sources, relevant cases were identified and further researched. Other strategies, as well, were used and proved to be quite helpful. Collegial input is a valuable asset to any project.

Using a theoretical framework and an operational definition of professional dissent, the interview schedule was designed using open-ended questions. Free-response questions worked well for us and should be employed in similar projects. The advantages of using this strategy outweigh the drawbacks. They are effective in revealing the informant's own definition of the situation, and the phrasing of open-ended questions is closer to that used in ordinary conversation.

If financial constraints are not severe, it is best to use two interviewers when dealing with sophisticated informants. The tandem interviewing method can exploit the informant's ability to the fullest extent. However, by using a tape recorder it is possible to compensate. Free from note taking, the interviewer is able to devote his or her full attention to the informant.

Telephone interviewing also proved to be an excellent substitute for the on-site visits. We found no significant response differences between those interviewed face-to-face and those interviewed over the telephone. Any information that can be asked in person can be investigated over the telephone, except for those questions requiring visual cues.

Finally, an assessment was made regarding the relative importance of the additional supporting evidence. Compared to the interviews with organizational informants, the supporting evidence was worthwhile for numerous reasons.

NOTES

We are indebted to Dr. David Duffee and Mr. George Capowich for their work in drafting sections 1 and 2 respectively of part A.

1. Robert Perrucci, Robert Anderson, Dan E. Schendel, and Leon E. Trachtman, "Whistle-blowing: Professionals' Resistance to Organizational Authority," Social Problems 28 (December 1980): 149-164.
2. James A. Waters, "Catch 20.5: Corporate Morality As An Organizational Phenomenon," Organizational Dynamics, (Spring 1978): 3-19.
3. Robert M. Anderson, Robert Perrucci, Dan E. Schendel, and Leon E. Trachtman, Divided Loyalties (West Lafayette, IN: Purdue University, 1980).
4. R. Merton, M. Fiske, and P.L. Kendall, The Focused Interview (New York: The Free Press, 1956); and Robert K. Merton and Patricia L. Kendall, "The Focused Interview," American Journal of Sociology 51 (1946): 541-557.
5. Lewis Anthony Dexter, Elite and Specialized Interviewing (Evanston, IL: Northwestern University Press, 1970).

6. Hans Toch, Agents of Change: A Study in Police Reform (New York: John Wiley and Sons, 1975); and Hans Toch, Living in Prison (New York, The Free Press, 1977).
7. See James H. Frey, Survey Research By Telephone (Beverley Hills, CA: Sage Publishers, 1983) for an excellent discussion of telephone surveys compared to face-to-face interviews. Pages 195-201 list useful references.
8. Anderson, et.al., Divided Loyalties.
9. Ralph H. Oates, "Differences in Responsiveness in Telephone Versus Personal Interviews," The Journal of Marketing 19 (October 1954): 169.
10. Joseph Hochstim, "Comparison of Three Information Gathering Strategies in a Population Study of Sociomedical Variables," Proceedings of the Social Statistics Section American Statistical Association, (1962): 154-159.
11. John Colombotos, "The Effects of Personal vs. Telephone Interviews on Socially Acceptable Responses," Paper presented at the Annual Meeting of the American Association for Public Opinion Research, Groton, CT, May 14, 1965.
12. Anderson, et.al., Divided Loyalties.
13. Ralph Nader, Peter J. Petkas, and Kate Blackwell, eds., Whistleblowing (New York: Grossman, 1972).
14. Alan F. Westin, Whistle Blowing: Loyalty and Dissent in the Corporation (New York: McGraw-Hill, 1981).
15. Greg Mitchell, Truth...And Consequences: Seven Who Would Not Be Silenced (New York: Dembner Books, 1981).

FIVE
RESEARCHERS AND
REPORTERS

In the course of gathering information on organization members we planned to interview, we stumbled into a moral dilemma that sharply divided the project staff: the issue was confidentiality, and it was raised by a question from a reporter. Since our topic was whistleblowing, we faced the anomalous and ironic prospect of blowing the whistle on whistleblowers, or having the whistle blown on us. The issue was not one on which any of the staff was neutral: a decision had to be made about the uses to which the information we had gathered could be put. Who should have access to our data and under what conditions? This is not a question to which we--or many other social researchers--could give one, unanimous answer, but it was critical to our project.[1]

SWAPPING INFORMATION

Both researchers and reporters are in the business of gathering and disseminating information. Typically, their techniques differ: researchers use the "scientific method", which imposes rigorous constraints on how information is gathered, analyzed, and presented; reporters work through more informal means--relying on telephone conversations, tips and rumors--and presenting their materials with more concreteness in order to engage a wider audience.

Both are careful to protect their sources.[2] One of our senior colleagues fondly pointed out that the First Amendment gives reporters more protection than it does to any scientific researcher. Because sources of information are guarded, they are difficult to get at--with the result that an exchange of information can become an attractive option.

One of our interviewees, at the end of our very first session and after the tape recorder had (at his request) been turned off, hinted at an illegal campaign contribution made by the head of an international petro-chemical company to the governor of a New England state. Though he was unwilling to be quoted for fear of retaliation, lawsuits, and dismissal, he suggested that a local newspaper had run stories that mentioned the connection, which he insisted was critical to understanding why he was fired. We then had the task of tracking down these stories, with only a vague time frame and hints of a headline to guide us.

As a way to avoid a hand-search of every newspaper for the 6-to 12-month period in question, we decided to contact a reporter at the local newspaper, hoping that he could recall the stories or check his own files. Each newspaper maintains a morgue of dead stories, a listing of coverage of individuals, organizations, and incidents, but only newspaper staff have access to the morgue. Clearly, it would be much more efficient to use the newspaper morgue to follow this lead, but also--as it turned out--more perilous.

What could we offer the reporter in exchange for his efforts and the information he might find? This question was quickly raised by the reporter in response to our request for cooperation. Our most attractive offer was reciprocal access to our own data. Thus, the possibility of swapping information arose; the reporter would provide us with all stories concerning the governor's relation to this chemical company, and we would provide the reporter with transcripts of interviews with those people who had agreed to be identified. Because of misgivings about such an exchange, this prospect was presented to the reporter only as a possibility, pending deliberations among the project staff.

SOME HURDLES

The proposal to exchange information was not well received by the project staff.[3] A variety of objections were voiced before we reached the heart of the matter.

Some objected because they did not like the idea. This objection was more a matter of sentiment than of principle, but nevertheless the objection was sincere and strong. Information swapping was thought to be in bad taste, a violation of professional etiquette, a breach of our professional roles as researchers. Horsetrading is not one of the activities in which researchers properly engage. The very prospect offends their professional dignity. It strikes some as vulgar to barter information. Primitive societies may engage in such activities but not a community of scholars. Merchants may haggle over the price of goods, but academics should not negotiate with their data.

This objection depends on seeing an exchange of information in an unfavorable light. If instead one characterizes it as the dissemination of knowledge, it is less reprehensible. If one sees reporters and researchers as each in the business of gathering and distributing information, then the exchange is a form of collaboration among professionals engaged in a common pursuit.

But though their objectives are similar, they are not the same--as some of the project staff insisted. It is in view of these differences that some project members objected to the exchange.

Reporters are not researchers. Though each may be in the information business, to say that they are the same struck some researchers as analogous to saying that humans and rats are the same--both are animals engaged in the business of securing their individual and collective survival. Reporters use different tools, aim at a different audience, and have different legal rights and a different code of ethics to shape and guide their work.

Conceding all this, one can still ask: Do these differences make a difference--specifically a moral difference? Raising this question helps to get us to the moral heart of the matter.

THE CONSENT ISSUE

It is now possible to articulate one moral objection to the exchange of information between reporters and researchers. As a fully developed argument, it could be stated as follows:

p^1 Use of the transcripts is restricted by the terms of consent;

P^2 No one consented to the release of the transcripts to reporters;

C The transcripts should not be released to reporters.

The argument could be reworded and tightened to make the reasoning more explicit. It would then have the following logical form:

$$(X) (XM \supset XC)$$
$$\frac{- C}{- M}$$

   In ordinary language this would read: for all X, X is
moral only if X is consented to; the exchange of information
with reporters was not consented to; hence, this exchange is
immoral. In its logical form this argument is called modus
tolens or denying the consequent. All arguments that fit
this form are valid—which means that the conclusion follows logically from the premises. In every valid argument,
if the premises are true, the conclusion must be true. But
the premises may or may not be true; that is a question of
fact. To assert that an argument is valid is to assert a logical relationship between the premises and the conclusion;
the conclusion cannot logically be false if the premises of
the argument are true. But are the premises true?
   Let us consider the first premise. What is the relationship between moral behavior and consent?
   Clearly, much of our conduct is right and good—even
though perhaps no one has consented to it. Here I refer not
just to actions that mainly affect the agent—such as going
to the dentist for regular checkups—but to actions that
affect others. Saving the life of someone who has not requested it is clearly the morally correct thing to do, even
though there is no contract to which people may consent.
   Social philosophers have attempted to save the preeminence of the consent doctrine by arguing for a tacit
social contract to which all give consent by their behavior.[4] Such a move is an effort to patch up a principle
that is already in jeopardy. Admittedly, if people were
given the option of consenting to be saved, they would agree
to it, but appeals to hypothetical or tacit consent would
make one suspect that another principle has come into play.
The effort to universalize consent as an absolute restriction on all moral conduct, to the exclusion of all other

principles, makes the first principle problematic. Efforts to save the first principle by appealing to tacit or hypothetical consent may become redundant when one considers the second premise.

For if there is any question of what people did or would consent to, there is a simple solution: Ask them! The second premise asserts as a fact--not as a principle--that people never agreed to have the information released to reporters. This is an empirical claim. One way to determine whether it is true or false is to read our consent form carefully. Those interviewed were given three options: to be identified by name, to be identified by role in a named organization, or to remain anonymous. Could we share transcripts of those who agreed to be identified by name?

If they agreed to be identified by name, have they agreed to our use of the transcripts in any fashion we choose? Not quite. The consent form states the general purposes of the research project and the anticipated products. Though it speaks of a case book, scholarly monographs, and articles in professional journals, it does not refer to newspaper stories. Arguably, people might be upset to read their names in a local newspaper, or equally arguable,they might be flattered--it could depend on what the reporter wrote. But their consent to such a use was not explicit; therefore, an assumption of tacit consent is problematic. So neither the first nor second premise can easily be proven to be true, but neither can they be easily proven false.

A COMPROMISE REJECTED

At this juncture we had reached an impasse. Several strategies were possible to resolve it. The easiest strategy was to ask each person if he or she would agree to release the transcripts to reporters. This procedure would resolve the factual question: What exactly did the people think they were consenting to when they signed the consent form? If each of them had no objection to releasing the transcript, who were we to say "Nay"? The answer quickly came back: We are researchers.

One of the staff members objected that even if those persons interviewed agreed to such an exchange, he would not. And this response pushed us once again into a question of first principles.

BENEFITS AND BURDENS

The staff member's response rationale stressed once again the differences between reporters and researchers. Though both are in the business of disseminating information, they do so by different means, to different audiences, and for different purposes. Reporters want the public to be informed about the events, actions, and policies that affect them. Their freedom to report events is predicated on the belief that a knowledgeable electorate is vital to the functioning of a democratic political system. Researchers, however, may act for non-political or political reasons. Paradigmatically, and in its purest form, their objective is not an informed public but the advancement of knowledge. They are not obliged to disseminate their findings generally, among those who might misinterpret or misuse them. It suffices if they share the fruits of their labors among their peers, since those similarly trained can best appreciate their meaning and significance.[5]

This counter-argument can be advanced more readily when researchers carry on their work using their own resources, but rarely, if ever, is this the case. Much research is carried on by private industry for their individual and (occasionally) collective interests. Other research is funded by the government, which in turn draws its resources from the general public.[6]

In view of this dependency of researchers on public funds, as our project was, an argument can be developed in defense of releasing the transcripts to reporters as follows:

P^1 Those who bear the burden of research should reap the benefits;

P^2 The public bears this burden;

C^1 The public should reap the benefit;

P^3 For the public to reap the benefit, their widest dissemination is required;

P^4 Releasing the transcripts helps ensure the widest dissemination;

C^2 The transcripts should be released.

As articulated in this fashion, two arguments are involved where the conclusion to the first is a premise of the second. The arguments could be tightened and made more precise. The first premise could be qualified to state that all those who bear some burden should receive some benefit, and the second premise could divide the public more precisely into beneficiaries and non-beneficiaries. But such efforts to be more precise would make for too much precision in an argument that relies on general principles for its force. To demand more precision would be like using the finely honed tools of the surgeon to chop down a tree: an ax will do, and we should not demand any more precision than the task at hand dictates. Accordingly, let us leave the argument in this admittedly rough form and ask: Is it a sound one?

The first conclusion follows logically from the premises, but both premises can be contested. One might object that not all members of the public bear this burden, and, clearly, this claim would be true. Those who pay no taxes because their age or income is too low do not bear any of the burden for this research. Yet such an objection might return to the earlier point of precision. And it may miscarry, for the issue is the availability of the benefits of the research to those who support it. The issue is whether the media serve as a suitable conduit for making this information generally available to anyone who might benefit from it.

The first premise would be false if it asserted that only those who supported such research should benefit from it. Taken in this restrictive sense, it would preclude any benefits to the needy or the meritorious, so that it can be plausibly taken to assert only that if one has borne some burden is one entitled to some benefit. There are restrictions on this principle. If I pay someone $100,000 to assassinate the President, I am not entitled to the alleged benefits arising from the President's death. I am not entitled to the benefits of illegal or immoral actions for which I bear the burden. Therefore, the first premise must be construed to govern an exchange of benefits and burdens that conform to standard legal and moral principles of justice.

Premise four is difficult to contest. Newspapers are, almost by definition, one of the mass media, one of the ways to communicate with a large number of people. Yet the principle could be contested. Imagine the following hypothetical scenario.

P^1 As the result of releasing the transcripts to reporters, others who might have agreed to be interviewed refuse;

P^2 As a result of the refusal of these few key individuals, no further cases can be studied;

C   The research has to be terminated.

According to this scenario, the project could be aborted because of a lack of cooperation. The two premises are conjectural and may stem more from fear than from fact. To the extent that data could be gathered to support them, the fourth premise could be contested.

It is also possible to take issue with the third premise. If one is inclined to elitism, where benefits are more a function of the application of knowledge by experts, then public dissemination is not nearly as important as scholarly publication. It is not newspapers that should then serve as a conduit for information but professional journals and meetings of academic groups, for only in the hands of the skilled, who are able to make use of knowledge, can its benefits be reaped.

To mount an argument that it is wrong, let us switch from these utilitarian considerations of benefits back to a deontological consideration of consent.

THE PROBLEM OF CONSENT REVISITED

The conflict between researchers and reporters arose initially because individuals had not consented explicitly to this use of the transcripts. Not only had some failed to agree because they had not been asked, they had refused to agree. Some of those interviewed explicitly requested that their names not be released; they did not want to be identified, not even indirectly by role. Our commitment of confidentiality to these people had to be respected.

Yet this commitment cannot be taken as an absolute prescription that would override all other considerations. Most people recognize that under some conditions a breach of confidence is warranted. Differences would probably arise not over the principle but over the particulars: How serious must the situation be before a breach can be morally justified?[7]

Some research staff were already familiar with one such situation. In the course of doing research on prisoners, promises of confidentiality were made to some of those interviewed, including correctional personnel. In the midst of their work, the researchers discovered that prisoners were being physically abused by prison guards. Should they blow the whistle on their subjects and report these beatings? To do so would violate promises that had been made and would lead to the termination of the project. Yet they did not hesitate to report the beatings because they believed the incidents were very serious.

In this situation the researchers have no option that would help them avoid wrongdoing. They are caught in a moral double-bind and can only choose between two evils, either to break a promise or to allow the beatings to continue. They must choose the lesser of the two.[8]

Our own project, however, was hardly in a moral crisis. As yet, we knew of no serious wrongdoing that could be caused solely by a breach of confidentiality. Instead of the lesser of two evils, we were weighing a possible good against a clear wrong. One difficulty encountered in this weighing process is a difference in the probabilities. To break a promise is definitely wrong--the probability of harm is very high--but the probable benefit from the dissemination of information through newspapers is not as high and is very difficult even to estimate accurately. Thus, the probability estimates vary markedly in degree and certainty. A second difficulty is that the wrongdoing is based on different moral principles. Breach of promise, it may be argued on Kantian or deontological ethical principles, is wrong regardless of the consequences because it violates a fundamental requirement of respect for persons. The social benefits that might accrue from greater publicity, however, depend very much on the actual consequences--the contingencies of circumstances. These benefits are appraised through experience rather than through principles. The seriousness of the moral wrong is difficult to weigh against the significance of the social benefit because we do not know how to make a calculation in which epistemological factors relate to moral principles and (to make matters worse) to different moral principles in this case.

Robert Nozick has provided one schema for dealing with conflicting moral principles.[9] He treats such deontological principles as respect for persons as secondary or side constraints in the pursuit of social goals. Accordingly, we might regard consent as posing a restriction on research, which could only be violated when some more fundamental right--such as the right to bodily integrity or life--is at issue. In the absence of such a right, no violation of consent could be justified in the name of the greater social good.

It might seem, then, that the solution to the initial dilemma would be to secure the explicit consent of each individual interviewed and release only those transcripts where such consent had been provided. Unfortunately, this strategy, however plausible it might seem, floundered as a result of a further problem.

INDIVIDUAL AND COLLECTIVE CONSENT

If each individual were an entity unto himself or herself, then securing each one's consent would relieve our moral quandary. Unfortunately, individuals are not isolated in this way, especially in large organizations where they interact in complex ways. As a result, we had to worry about breaching the confidence of an informant inadvertently and indirectly by identifying him through what others had said. If everyone agreed to have his or her identity revealed and his or her statements publicly disseminated, no moral problem would exist. At the other extreme, if everyone refused to reveal his or her identity and insisted on complete anonymity, our prima facie moral obligation is clear. But how should we act when some consent but others do not?

We have to be concerned that we do not accidentally breach someone's trust. Admittedly, to do so unintentionally is not as serious a moral transgression as to do so deliberately. But recklessness can still be a serious moral (and legal) fault. Once we became aware of the possibility of indirect disclosure, a moral responsibility was placed upon us to take some measures to safeguard our subjects.

In practice several options were available to us. One extreme solution was to delete all references to those who asked that their identities not be revealed. One might assume that if they were never mentioned by name, anonymity would be secured. This assumption is false, for if they are identified by office, and it is a matter of public record that they occupied that office, modest detective work would easily identify them as the source of information they had asked us to keep confidential. Accordingly, it would not suffice that only their names be deleted. It may additionally be necessary that they not be identified by role. Would this suffice?

We could not be certain that it would. Conceivably there might be some information to which only the individual occupying a particular role in the organization would have access. Though the source of this confidential information were not identified by name or role, an energetic detective or reporter could locate the source using other materials and identify the informant in this way. Thus, we would inadvertently have committed a wrong we did not intend.[10]

The most dramatic solution to this problem would require all names to be deleted--the names of individuals, organizations, the state, and titles of offices. It was to this solution that we were eventually driven as the result of issues raised by the reporter.[11] Only such a drastic measure would be certain to protect the identities of those who had spoken to us in confidence.

NOTES

We would like to thank Dr. Mark S. Frankel for helpful references to the social science literature pertinent to this chapter.

1. For a general discussion of confidentiality in social research, see the following works; J.A. Barnes, Who Should Know What: Social Science, Privacy and Ethics (New York: Cambridge, 1979); Tom Beauchamp, R.R. Faden, R.J. Wallace, Jr. and L. Walters (eds), Ethical Issues in Social Science Research (Baltimore, MD: John Hopkins University Press, 1982).
2. For a general discussion of protecting the sources, see R.F. Boruch, and J.S. Cecil, Assuring the Confidentiality of Data in Social Research (Philadelphia: University of Pennsylvania Press, 1979). For an insightful discussion of the extent to which some researchers in criminal justice go, see Marvin Wolfgang "Ethics and Research" in Ethics, Public Policy and Criminal Justice eds. F.A. Elliston and N. Bowie (Cambridge, MA: Oelgeschlager, Gunn and Haine, 1982), pp. 391–417.
3. Some of these reasons are discussed by other researchers in the following works: T. Dalenius and A. Klevmarken (eds), Personal Integrity and the Need for Data in the Social Sciences (Stockholm: Swedish Council for Social Science Research, 1976). Mark S. Frankel, "Ethics and Responsibility in Political Science Research," International Social Science Journal 30 (1978): 173–180; E. Diener and R. Crandall, Ethics in Social and Behavioral Research (Chicago: University of Chicago Press, 1978).
4. For an historical treatment of this doctrine, see Ernest Barker's The Social Contract (New York: Oxford University Press, 1960). The most notable contemporary philosopher to use it is John Rawls. See A Theory of Justice (Cambridge, MA: Harvard University Press, 1971).
5. This rather elitist view of the role of the social scientist can conflict with both law, morality and the political machinery. See Paul Nejelski (ed), Social Research in Conflict with Law and Ethics (Cambridge, MA: Ballinger Publishing Co., 1976); P.D. Reynolds, Ethics and Social Science Research (Englewood Cliffs, NJ: Prentice Hall, 1982).
6. The role of government in social research is discussed in G. Sjoberg (ed), Ethics, Politics and Social Research (Cambridge, MA: Schenkman Publishing Co., 1967).

7. See Richard DeGeorge's useful discussion of this issue in "Whistleblowing: Permitted, Prohibited, Required," in Conflicting Loyalties in the Workplace, ed. F. A. Elliston (Notre Dame: University of Notre Dame Press, 1984.)

8. Carl Klockars has dramatized this problem forcefully and eloquently in a classic paper in police science. See "The Dirty Harry Problem," in Moral Issues in Police Work, eds. F. A. Elliston and M. Feldberg (Totowa, NJ: Rowman and Allenheld, 1984).

9. See Robert Nozick Anarchy, State and Utopia (New York: Basic Books, 1974).

10. For a discussion of some of the moral issues raised by such accidents, see K. Studer, and D. E. Chubin, "Ethics and the Unintended Consequences of Social Research: A Perspective from the Sociology of Science," Policy Sciences 8 (1977): 111-124.

11. See Chapter Six (this volume) for further discussions of this question.

SIX
CONSTRUCTING
FICTIONALIZED
CASES

THE QUESTION OF CONFIDENTIALITY

In survey research and public opinion polls, informants are often given a guarantee of anonymity, that is, the researcher does not know the identity of the informant. This is done on the premise that anonymity assures frank and revealing answers. On the other hand, confidentiality means that the informant's identity will be protected. The researcher knows the informant but promises not to disclose his or her identity if requested. No data obtained in an interview will be traceable to a particular individual in the event of publication.

During the initial months of our project, informants had three options regarding confidentiality: to be identified by name, to be identified only by role in a named organization, or to be identified by role in an unnamed organization.

By giving them the freedom to choose from among these options, we created a number of dilemmas for ourselves. Suppose, for example, that Mr. A, the president of Corporation X, said we could identify him by name. At this point there is no problem since he is our first organizational informant. However, we then interview Mr. B, the general counsel, who requests that he not be identified by name but rather by only a role in an unnamed organization. Already there is a conflict. By identifying Mr. A in the case write-up, we, in essence, are identifying Corporation X, a violation of Mr. B's consent form, if Mr. B's responses are included in the account. One could easily discover the identity of the corporation with little effort and research, using one of the corporation directories.

To take this example even further, suppose we interview the personnel director, Ms. C, who decides that she will allow us to identify her by role in a named organization. Her option is congruent with Mr. A's, but again conflicts with Mr. B's. By naming the organization, we would not be respecting Mr. B's request. Moreover, if Ms. C is the only personnel director at Corporation X, then through the identification of her role, her guarantee of confidentiality is compromised. Similarly, where there are only two people in a particular organizational position, their responses cannot be reported separately, unless they are both willing to be identified by name. Likewise, other information has to be considered so that an informant's identity is held in confidence. For example there will be few middle-level managers in Corporation X who attended Harvard University, are married with five children, and who came from the South.

Returning to our original example, we now have three informants within the same corporation who have exercised the full range of options. Extensive interviewing within Corporation X would continue to compound the problem. The situation just described did in fact occur.

Several possible remedies existed. First, we could have elected not to use the responses of those persons who, like Mr. B, did not wish to be identified in a named organization, thereby incorporating responses from the remaining informants into the case studies. However, this alternative would not be totally satisfactory. In omitting someone's perspective, critical points may be lost. Second, we could have chosen to identify all informants by only a role in unnamed organizations. This strategy also offered disadvantages. All of our primary informants (whistleblowers) wanted to be identified by name. One whistleblower, in particular, went so far as to state that he would not participate in our study if he were not identified by name. No assurances were given, and the informant finally consented to the interview. However, this could have been a problem since the whistleblower's contribution is significant. Additionally, something is lost when the organization is not identified. Although it is not necessary for sociological purposes, identifying the organization and the characters involved enhances the reality of the situation. Supporting evidence and previous discussions of the case can be included in the account; the reader can be referred to additional sources for documentation of the facts presented in the analysis.

This dilemma was solved for us during the final stages of our project. The Institutional Review Board decided, upon a second review, that the information disclosed by the informants and subsequently reported could lead to reprisals against the informant or third party human subjects named in the interview, or to a libel suit against the Criminal Justice Research Center. As a result, the previous three options had to be deleted from the consent form. In their place was a phrase (see page 63) that guaranteed that all names, titles, or other identifying information of actual persons or organizations would not be used in any book or article. This new requirement meant that the case accounts would have to be fictionalized.

A related point needs to be elaborated here. In fictionalizing cases one must not only consider names and titles, but the whistleblowing event itself, especially in the more well-known cases. For example if one were studying the case of the federal employee who blew the whistle on the C5-A cargo plane, merely deleting the name of the organization and fictionalizing informants' names would not suffice. Anyone knowledgeable about the event would realize that it was Ernest Fitzgerald of the Defense Department. Similarly, how many FDA doctors blew the whistle on the swine flu program? Only one, Dr. Anthony Morris. Therefore, one has to attend to these details too.

FICTIONALIZATION

In survey research, the researcher reports his or her findings quantitatively—61 percent of 250 respondents believe that abortions should be legal. The identity of those persons interviewed is not disclosed in the research report. However, a fieldworker cannot always guarantee such anonymity. The organization that we study, for instance, had only one president, one general counsel, and one personnel director.

One solution is to use fictitious names for the organization, the city where it is located, and for all of the role incumbents mentioned. Presumably, therefore, the identities of the informants will be protected. Readers external to the organization may be unable to associate statements with names, but what about those readers who are members of the organization? The researcher's name is familiar to organizational members and will be most likely be on the published report. In the case account it may be necessary to mention that the president of corporation X is perceived by staff to engage in unethical behavior and characterized as having an authoritarian leadership style. Several organizational secrets may be subsequently disclosed in the write-up of the case, and organizational members knowledgeable of the study will be able to identify key informants. While the interviewer for our study was in one of the host organizations, an informant boasted that he could identify key respondents in a previous research project conducted at his organization.

One other solution is to publish field studies under pseudonyms. But because of the prestige involved in doing research and the fact that colleges and universities emphasize scholarly inquiry, researchers want recognition for their work

Another remedy is to wait several years to publish the research report Some researchers do this in the belief that controversial findings will no longer be sensitive or that organizational members will then be scattered. However, this answer does not suffice in all cases. In order for research findings to have an impact on policy decisions, the results must be reported in a timely fashion

A final alternative is to change the concrete details surrounding the case so that it is unrecognizable to organizational informants. But as we shall see in the later discussion, this option poses difficult questions. Given that certain details are crucial, the researcher is almost forced to include the information. Researchers must continually make decisions on what to publish and what to omit in their accounts.

Fictionalization is commonly used in social research, yet the literature on the subject is sparse. At most, researchers simply acknowledge that they have assigned fictitious names to their characters. Oftentimes, the organization's name and location are left intact. For example in Agents of Change, Dr. Hans Toch discusses his project with the Oakland Police Department. In using excerpts from tape-recorded sessions in his book, Dr. Toch fictionalized the police officers' names. However, in the acknowledgments he disclosed their true identities. Also included is a foreword by the chief of police, also a participant in the study.[1]

In William Whyte's classic Streetcorner Society, Whyte fictionalized not only the names of his informants, but the name of the town that he studied. Even with these changes, Whyte recognized a remaining problem. He noted if he (the researcher) disguises the name of the district as I have done, many outsiders apparently will not discover where the study was actually located. The people in the district, of course, know it is about them, and even the changed names do not disguise the individuals for them.[2]

Oral historians and anthropologists also employ this strategy to protect a subject's identity. In First Person America, Ann Banks states that she provided fictitious names for the life histories collected by the Federal Writers Project some 40 years ago.[3] Similarly, Marjorie Shostak, an anthropologist, who recently published an oral history, assigned a pseudonym to her informant because the tribeswoman Nisa gave her explicit details about her love life and sex life.[4] Ms. Shostak states: "I considered it respectful, and a way of protecting Nisa from people in her society, who might object to her discussion."[5]

With these discussions in mind, as well as our own common sense, we embarked upon the task of fictionalizing the cases--a most difficult process.

TELLING STORIES

I am beginning to believe that nothing can ever be proved. These are honest hypotheses that take the facts into account: but I sense so definitely that they come from me, and that they are simply a way of unifying my knowledge . . . Slow, lazy, sulky, the facts adapt themselves to the rigor of the order I wish to give them but it remains outside of them. I have the feeling of doing a work of pure imagination.[6]

In this early semi-autobiographical work, Sartre, describes his difficulty in recounting the life of another. He began on the assumption that he was just recording the facts, but in his efforts to substantiate and organize these facts according to some principle or set of principles, he found himself involved in a world of the imagination.

In fictionalizing the materials on our project, it was necessary to change more than the names. Tell-tale evidence could easily be contained in some of the facts provided. Those who are familiar with scandals and exposes could recognize a famous incident from the story that was told. To change the names without changing the incriminating evidence would stop short of all that could be done to protect the identity of our informants. Accordingly, we found it necessary, in the name of confidentiality, to tell a story, to invent a new story. But what story, or what kind of story?

The interviews themselves did not provide a univocal answer to this question. They did not dictate a story--or perhaps more accurately, they did not dictate any single story. They told many, too many, stories. Each person interviewed was asked about an incident in which there was a difference of professional opinion, but they did not select the same incident. Even if they had, we would not have been able to use it if it allowed our informants to be identified. Out of the interviews, the newspaper accounts, the annual reports and the published materials, we had to tell a story--one that made sense of the materials, one that made a point, and one that concealed the identity of our informants.

Different kinds of stories could be told. Reviewing the cases as they are written, four distinct types emerge. These reflect the orientation of the authors, perhaps their training or personal life history. None of them do violence to the facts, but at the same time they are not demanded by them either. They go beyond the facts, into the world of fantasy.

The Triumph of Man

Whistleblowers are people who encounter obstacles. They have a goal in mind--to warn someone or some organization, to help achieve something worthwhile for a company, a group or perhaps a country. But significant achievements are seldom easy, and professionals must struggle to reach their goals. They must fight against the biases of others, their conflicting values, and perhaps their false beliefs. One kind of story is a success story: the individual's triumph over the odds to win a measure of victory. People may lose, but if they are courageous, honest, and optimistic, they can find that they have wrestled something of value even in their defeat. The success story is one story to tell.

The Pragmatic Point of View

In each of the cases studied, some strategy was used in an effort to resolve the conflicting professional judgments. Some of these strategies worked well and others did not--depending on the range of opportunities and resources available, what the individual sought to achieve, and how adept the individual was at using the means or strategy employed. One can tell a story focused on the strategy, adopting a practical or pragmatic perspective. Whereas the first approach emphasizes the determination, courage, and resilience of the individual, this second approach emphasizes the appropriateness of the means used to achieve the individual's end. One tells a story not of personal triumph, but a lesson about what works and what does not work.

The Moralist's Approach

Behind the perspective of each individual is a set of personal values. Some of these are purely prudential and self-serving, some are ideological or political and serve the interests of a special group, and others are ethical or moral, taking justice or the social good as the final court of appeal. The conflicts in the drama can be represented as moral conflicts--competing judgments about what is right and what is wrong. The approach of the moralist highlights these conflicts in moral values. The moralist may simply try to bring these into sharper focus, or the moralist may try to resolve them. Such a resolution can be achieved in several ways. The value system of an individual can be attacked as internally inconsistent--generating incompatible demands. Or one person's values can be shown to violate generally accepted principles such as the golden rule, the prohibition on harming the innocent, or the injunction to maximize the social good.

The God's-Eye View

Success stories, to be compelling and dramatic, usually adopt the point of view of the individual--in our case the whistleblower. The success story is told from this person's point of view, or at least this person is made the central protagonist. But as fiction, psychoanalysis, and phenomenology have demonstrated, personal perspectives do not always agree. In an effort to capture these disagreements in a way that is both fair and accurate, the story can be narrated from the point of view of a disinterested and omniscient bystander--thereby offering a kind of God's-eye view of events. The emphasis falls not on personal triumph but on objectivity, comprehensiveness, and neutrality.

STYLE VERSUS SUBSTANCE

In the interviews people told their own stories in their own words. But when these interviews were transcribed, the results did not always do people justice. Their occasional eloquence could be masked by embarrassing pauses, and the reader could be distracted by unintended asides or false starts. Thus, we decided that we would clean up the transcripts, edit them slightly. But on what principles should this editorial work be based?

Several factors motivated and guided these emendations. First and foremost, we were concerned with accuracy; we did not want to change anything that would lead to to a misrepresentation of what someone had said. Since the interviews had been taped, it was always possible to verify the accuracy of the transcription. In revising the transcript, the first task was to eliminate any errors that had crept in as the result of our own work. This editing was a simple task of eliminating typographical errors that we had made. Beyond the typographical errors were factual inaccuracies that needed to be corrected--the wrong name of a company or person, an incorrect date or statistic.

Second, we wanted a transcript that was readable. Lengthy pauses and uninformative repetitions can be wearying on the staff who are studying the transcripts. A series of distracting "ahs" and "ummms" can make reading tedious. It was tempting to omit these from the transcript in order to ease our work. Yet when we did so, we went beyond style into substance; pauses and repetitions are indicative of an uncertain or redundant mind and to eliminate these alters the reader's picture of the speaker. These revisions mark a shift from style to substance.

The boundary between the two is hard to mark. Consider another judgment call: Where do you insert the period? People do not always speak in sentences, and the punctuation used to divide their words reflects a judgment call on what they would have said in the written as opposed to the spoken medium. The editors do no intentional harm with their best guess. But what about long rambling sentences strung together with a series of "ands?" Here again, in order to ease our work, it is tempting to change the style somewhat--to divide the longer sentence up into smaller ones that are more readable. But once again, this change represents a shift from style to substance. It alters not just how the person interviewed speaks but the readers' image of that person. A third example illustrates the same issue--ungrammatical sentences. These can be tedious and annoying to a reader who takes pride in speaking the King's English as it was meant to be spoken. People who are careless with their linguistic heritage can antagonize more respectful speakers. But again, to clean up the transcripts by making them grammatical alters the image of the speaker.

Fortunately, in all three cases there is a middle ground. One of the advantages of word processors is that with four key stokes one can copy an entire transcript-- preserving the original with all its flaws. One has an accurate, even if annoying, copy of exactly, what was said.

What are the limits on what we can do with what was said? Since we were fictionalizing the cases, were we required to quote people's words exactly or could we take liberties with them? Can we misrepresent a fictitious speaker?

Again it was necessary to draw lines along a continuum. To alter a word, eliminate a pause, or correct the grammar when one is citing a fictitious speaker could enhance the dramatic impact without distorting the greater truth. Such changes may help to make the speaker's point in a more compelling and forceful way. Without exactly placing unintended words in a speaker's mouth, one can place better words-- words that are clearer, more grammatical, more cogent. One can have the fictionalized speaker say what the real speaker would have said if he or she had just thought of that better way to put it. It is tempting to take the liberty of making the fictitious speaker more eloquent. Here we sacrifice the literal truth for drama and the greater truth.

NOTES

1. Hans Toch, J. Douglas Grant, and Raymond T. Galvin, Agents of Change: A Study in Police Reform. (New York: John Wiley & Sons, 1975).
2. William Foote Whyte, Streetcorner Society. (Chicago: University of Chicago Press, 1955).
3. Ann Banks, ed, First-Person America. (New York: Alfred A. Knopf, 1980), p. xxiii.
4. Marjorie Shostak, Nisa: The Life and Words of a !Kung Woman (Cambridge, MA: Harvard University Press, 1981).
5. Karen J. Winkler, "Transferring Spoken Words to Print: The Problems of the Oral History Book," The Chronicle Of Higher Education 24 (February 1982), p. 20.
6. Jean-Paul Sartre, Nausea (New York: New Directions, 1965), p. 13.

PART THREE
EMPIRICAL
ANALYSES

SEVEN
A LEGAL
ANALYSIS

Within recent years scholars have tended to view whistleblowing as a legitimate activity, while the majority of employers still characterize it as a disloyal act.[1] Developing concurrently with this debate is a parallel awareness of the harm to the environment and to the public health and safety originating from corporate violations or bureaucratic bungling. One only has to recall the kepone controversy in Virginia to be reminded of this.[2]

By bringing such activities to light, a whistleblower is often viewed in contradictory terms. To some he is seen as a champion, a courageous individual. To others he is a squealer, stool-pigeon, or "rat fink." Whatever the motivation, employees who choose to sound the alarm to call attention to their organization's wrongdoing jeopardize their livelihood, friendships, professional relationships, and opportunity for promotions and advancement. Although legislative enactments and codes of ethics embody an obligation to protect the public interest, whistleblowers are transferred, demoted, ostracized, and even fired when they attempt to fulfill this obligation.

Limited protections are available to dissenting employees. Federal anti-reprisal statutes are designed to insulate employees from retaliation. Arbitration and grievance procedures provide individuals who work under collective bargaining agreements with avenues to redress unjust dismissals. Whistleblower protection laws, which limit an employer's right to fire at will, have been passed by several state legislatures. And a handful of state courts are providing a remedy for those employees whose discharge violates some recognized public policy.

The courts are frequently invoked when there are two types of wrongdoing involved. First, there is the wrongdoing about which the whistleblower has voiced a concern. Second, this initial wrongdoing is compounded by the retaliatory action leveled against the employee for blowing the whistle in the first place. The whistleblower, in essence, is subjected to a second wrongdoing as a result of his or her dissent, either internally or externally.

This chapter examines the employee's legal rights to disclose wrongdoing. First, the employment at will doctrine is examined in several recent court decisions. Second, public employees' First Amendment rights of freedom of speech and petition are examined, along with other constitutional and statutory protections. Third, the numerous federal and state regulations governing the employment relationship are reviewed, including anti-reprisal provisions and recent whistleblower bills. Finally, the goals of the Civil Service Reform Act and the Inspector General Act are outlined, and the Merit Systems Protection Board and Office of Special Counsel are evaluated.

THE COURTS

The Private Sector

The employment-at-will doctrine is based on the premise that the employment contract is presumed to be terminable at will by either party at any time and for any reason. Therefore, the common law permits an employer to dismiss his employees at will even for "cause morally wrong" without being guilty of any wrongdoing.[3]

Two presumptions of law are involved. First, without a contract as to the duration of employment, the only obligation upon which to base the contractual obligation is work for pay.[4] Second, according to Justice Harlan in Adair vs. United States,[5] "the right of the employee to quit the service of the employer, for whatever reason, is the same as the right of the employer, for whatever reason, to dispense with the services of such employee." The relationship rests upon the concept of freedom of contract.

The origin of this doctrine can be traced to the development of laissez-faire capitalism in the latter half of the nineteenth century. This rule was well suited to "the rustic simplicity of the days when the farmer or small entrepreneur . . . was the epitome of American individualism,"[6] and by the early part of the twentieth century, this rule of law was widely accepted by American courts.[7]

Within recent years, however, a handful of state courts have created a notable exception to the employment-at-will doctrine.[8] Its origin is found in the court decision of Petermann vs International Brotherhood of Teamsters.[9] The court ruled that the right of an employer to discharge an at-will employee must be limited "by considerations of public policy."[10] Petermann involved an employee who refused to commit perjury before a state legislative committee and alleged that the only reason for his termination was in retaliation for his refusal to give false testimony. The California Court of Appeals held that the termination gave rise to a cause of action for wrongful discharge.[11]

Subsequent cases that have developed the public policy exception tend to fall into one of three categories, depending on the source of the determinant of public policy.[12] First, a statute may impute a right to the discharged employee and a corresponding duty, yet remain silent about the means of enforcing that right. The courts must determine if the statute intends that a private remedy be implied when an employer has attempted to contravene public policy.[13] Second, a statute may express a public policy that the employer has breached, but provide neither a right nor remedy for the terminated at-will employee. It is then up to the courts to imply both a right and a remedy.[14] Third, in the absence of legislative expression of a public policy covering the circumstances of the discharged employee, the employee must seek judicial implication of a right and a remedy. In this category the judiciary must also define public policy.[15]

The employee is required to show that through the use of retaliatory discharge power, the employer has breached societal interests through a violation of public policy. However, private at-will employees who have been dismissed for blowing the whistle on their organizations or refusing to engage in illegal or unethical conduct have not generally fared well in the courts. Several recent court cases illustrate the courts' application of this common law principle. Geary vs. United States Steel Co. [16] exemplifies the present attitude toward discharged whistleblowers. Geary, with 14 years of experience, attempted to have what he considered to be an unsafe product removed from the market. In doing so he contacted both customers and high corporate executives in U.S. Steel.[17] After his dismissal, he brought suit against U.S. Steel, alleging that his dismissal was wrongful, retaliatory, and against public policy.[18] On appeal the Pennsylvania Supreme Court sustained the dismissal of his action noting that a report of unsafe products was a legitimate reason for the discharge.[19]

In Percival vs. General Motors Corporation [20] Percival brought an action against his employer, alleging that his employment had been terminated in retaliation for his efforts to correct false securities representations given by General Motors to outside business associates.[21] The court concluded that the discharge of an employee for an attempt to correct false and misleading information about possible violation of securities laws conveyed to the public by his employer did not involve a breach of public policy sufficient to sustain a cause of action.[22]

Only 13 jurisdictions recognize a cause of action in tort for wrongful discharge.[23] According to Alfred Feliu,[24] these courts, after considering the merits of the case, have weighed four factors in their decision: 1) the importance of the relevant public policy;[25] 2) the place and context in which it was announced;[26] 3) how it fares when weighed against the employer's and society's broader interests;[27] and 4) whether the violation of the public policy in the case was so offensive as to warrant an exception to the employment-at-will doctrine.[28]

The Public Sector

The substantive rights of public employees to make disclosures originate from two sources--constitutional guarantees of freedom of speech and federal and state statutes that bar dismissal of employees except where a reason has been identified. Furthermore, employers must adhere to certain procedural requirements when formally sanctioning dissenting employees.

The courts originally adopted a very narrow view of the employment relationship in regard to the First Amendment rights of public employees. Employers could dismiss employees virtually at will. The traditional rationale was that public employment was a privilege conferred by the government on its own terms, and the public employee was doomed to accept the accompanying restrictions on his constitutional rights.[29] The right-privilege doctrine was enunciated by Justice Holmes in McAuliffe vs. Mayor of New Bedford.[30] In reviewing the case of McAuliffe, a policeman who had been fired for violating a regulation that limited his political activities, Justice Holmes commented: "The petitioner may have a constitutional right to talk politics, but he has no constitutional right to be a policeman."[31]

In the 50s and 60s, the Supreme Court began to modify the right-privilege doctrine. In Pickering vs. Board of

Education,[32] the Court held that public employment cannot be conditioned on a loss of constitutional rights. Pickering, a public school teacher, wrote a letter to the editor of a local newspaper that criticized the school board's allocation of funds. To resolve Pickering's claim to constitutional protection, the Court weighed the interest of the plaintiff in commenting on matters of public concern as a citizen against the interests of the state, his employer, in promoting the efficiency of its public services.[33] The Court held that because his employment was only tangentially related, his statements could not constitute grounds for dismissal.[34] This decision made it possible for a broad interpretation of public employees' First Amendment rights. For example more recent court decisions indicate that policy-making officials enjoy more limited protection than non-policymakers.[35] The rationale for this trend is that critical comments by high-level policymakers are more likely to disrupt the governmental process than those made by lower-level employees. Overall courts have applied the Pickering dicta to subsequent cases with unpredictable results. Thus, the First Amendment protection afforded public employees is still vague and varies with each case and court.

In addition to the constitutional guarantee of freedom of speech, a public employee enjoys a First Amendment right to petition. In Swaaley vs. United States,[36] the Court of Claims held that a navy shipyard mechanic who was dismissed for writing to the secretary of labor about improper promotions was entitled to damages.[37] Employees are extended the First Amendment protection so long as their critical statements are made in the course of a petition submitted to an agency superior whom the employee believes has the power to redress his grievance, and as long as the statements are not made with knowledge of their falsity or reckless disregard for the truth.[38]

Similarly, legislative enactments in the form of statutes offer protections to employees who petition Congress. For example under section 7102 of Title V of the United States Code, an employee is granted the right to speak to Congress, a committee, or a particular member.[39] However, the scope of this protection is unclear. Section 1505 of Title XVIII provides criminal sanctions for reprisals taken against employees who testify before Congress. Unlike section 7102, it is applicable only when Congress requests the testimony. It does not protect an employee who voluntarily makes his or her information known. Disclosures not taking the form of petitions to Congress are protected by sections 7501(a) and 7512(a) of Title V.[40]

Finally, procedural protections available to public employees are constitutional and statutory in nature. To invoke the constitutional guarantee of the due process clause, an employee must show that the reprisal involved a deprivation of the liberty or property right.[41] In Fitzgerald vs. Hampton[42] the Court held that Fitzgerald's statutory employment rights were within the liberty and concept of the Fifth Amendment,[43] thus the due process guarantee was interpreted to require that the hearing be open to the public and press. Although this was an administrative hearing of a quasi-judicial character, the public had an interest in the circumstances surrounding his dismissal after his testimony concerning the C5-A cost overruns.

Statutory protections under section 7502(a) or 7512(a)[44] make it mandatory that sanctioned employees be provided notice of adverse action(s) about to be taken, the reasons, an opportunity to rebut the notice in writing or in person, and notice of the agency's final determination.[45] Moreover, agency regulations and state statutes have granted additional important concessions to the employee; for example, some allow hearings to be open to the public,[46] while others mandate that the hearing be held before the effective date of termination.[47]

GOVERNMENT REGULATIONS

As the above discussion suggests, the employment relationship is subject to regulation by federal, state and local governments. Employers are prohibited from discharging or disciplining employees for numerous reasons.[48] The earliest federal statute to protect employees from unjust dismissals is the National Labor Relations Act (NLRA), enacted in 1935.[49] Section 7 guarantees to employees the right "to engage in . . . concerted activities for the purpose of collective bargaining or other mutual aid protections" in industries affecting interstate commerce.[50] Most collective bargaining agreements under the NLRA mandate "just cause" for dismissal. Similarly, approximately 15 states have adopted laws applicable to private employers, while 32 states have adopted statutes granting public employees the right to organize.[51]

Nonunion employees have received numerous guarantees from Congress in a piecemeal fashion, beginning with Title VII of the Civil Rights Act of 1964.[52] This act makes it an unlawful employment practice to discharge employees because of their race, color, religion, sex, or national origin. The federal Age Discrimination in Employment Act[53] protects employees between the ages of 40 and 70 against discrimination in employment. Most states have similar laws and

statutes prohibiting discrimination on the basis of other
attributes, such as handicap or marital status.[54]
 Furthermore, several recent federal statutes contain
anti-reprisal provisions. Congress enacted these special
employee protection provisions because of the growing concern for unchecked employer discriminatory power. Proponents
of such legislation argue that unless whistleblowers are
protected, serious health and safety violations will go unex-
posed. These statutes fall into two categories: occupational health and safety legislation and environmental laws.
The former category includes the Occupational Safety and
Health Act (OSHA), [55] Federal Mine Safety and Health
Act,[56] Longshoremen's and Harbor Workers Act,[57] and the
Atomic Energy Act.[58] Examples of the latter category
include the Federal Water Pollution Control Act,[59] the
Water Pollution Control Act,[60] the Resource Conservation
and Recovery Act,[61] the Toxic Substances Control Act,[62]
the Clean Air Act,[63] and the Surface Mining Reclamation
Act.[64] Employees are protected when they bring violations
to the attention of the appropriate authorities. Any employee who believes that he or she has been discriminated
against by an employer may file a complaint alleging such
discrimination with the Department of Labor, but the employee frequently has only 30 days in which to file.[65]
 Aside from this very short filing period, there are
other weaknesses. Using OSHA as an example, the deficiencies
will become apparent. Only OSHA can bring action in court
against the employer.[66] Additionally, it can settle with
the employer, with or without employee consent. There are
usually significant delays in the disposition of cases due
to backlogged files and limited staff. Even if the complaint
is investigated in a timely fashion, the act does not mandate that an employee be reinstated or that an employer
cease the allegedly retaliatory action while the case is
pending. Finally, critics argue that the penalties for OSHA
violations are not severe enough to deter future wrongdoing
because punitive damages are prohibited. The employer's
punishment is limited to reinstatement and the awarding of
back pay to the employee. These provisions need to be
strengthened in order to be more effective.
 A few states have enacted laws prohibiting discrimination against employees because of their political activities,[67] acceptance of jury duty,[68] or refusal to take a
lie detector test.[69] Moreover, several states have
recently passed "whistleblower bills" that forbid employers
to take reprisals against employees who report violation of
the law to authorities.[70]
 Michigan's whistleblower bill, enacted in early 1981,
is the first in the nation to protect both private and pub-

lic employees. It forbids employers to take reprisals against any employee who has given or is about to give information to authorities concerning possible violations of the law. Any employee who believes that an employer has violated the act may commence an action in circuit court. Once in court the employee has to prove that the employer did indeed fire or otherwise discriminate against him or her because he or she blew the whistle. If the court finds in the employer's favor, it could order the employee reinstated along with the payment of back wages, full reinstatement of fringe benefits and seniority rights, payment of actual damages, or any combination of these. Should the judge find in favor of the employer, he or she could order the employee to pay court costs including the employer's legal fees. A person who violates this act is subject to a civil fine of not more than $500.

The Maryland law, enacted in July 1980, empowers the state secretary of personnel to bring sanctions against any manager who attempts to take reprisals against a public employee for disclosing information either publicly or privately. The law, however, does not require any investigation into the underlying charges of wrongdoing--an apparent weakness.

A measure passed by California in 1979 offers protection only to those whistleblowers who testify before special legislative committees, thus offering limited protection. It is still too early to tell whether these laws will be effective in protecting employees.

REFORM LEGISLATION

Civil Service

In 1978 the Civil Service Commission was abolished by the Civil Service Reform Act.[71] The initiative was an awareness of the difficulties simultaneously encountered by the commission as a result of its conflicting responsibilities; to manage personnel and to protect employees. This conflict resulted in the creation of three new agencies: the Federal Labor Relations Authority (FLRA), the Merit Systems Protection Board (MSPB), and the Office of Personnel Management (OPM).

The Federal Labor Relations Authority acts as a referee in labor-management disputes. To stay abreast of unfair labor practices cases, the FLRA encourages informal, lower-level settlements.

The OPM, on the other hand, handles appeals and takes care of hiring, promotions, pay, and other personnel functions. Sponsors of the reform bill thus hoped to separate personnel management from the handling of employee complaints and judgment of violations.

The third element of President Carter's civil service reform plan, the MSPB, handles employees' complaints and tries to protect government whistleblowers who expose wrongdoing. Within the framework of the new board, the Office of Special Counsel (OSC) was established on January 11, 1979, by the Reorganization Plan No 2 of 1978, and its responsibilities were subsequently expanded under the Civil Service Reform Act.[72]

The board and the special counsel were given separate authorities and responsibilities. The OSC is a semi-autonomous office. Since the establishment of these offices, however, a number of questions regarding the relationship between the board and the special counsel have been raised. The special counsel does have regulatory and management control over its operations, but does not have independent budget authority.

A conflict arose in July 1980 when Congress reduced the OSC's $4.5 million budget by $2 million, virtually stopping all business. The following month Ruth Prokop, chairwoman of the MSPB, notified the acting special counsel of MSPB's intention to suspend all delegations of authority previously provided, including administrative responsibility for hiring and other personnel actions.[73] The OSC did not follow the directives issued by the MSPB, and, as a consequence, the MSPB filed suit against the acting special counsel asking the U.S. District Court for the District of Columbia to rule on the independence of the special counsel's office. It is not known if or when the court will rule on this case; it may be dismissed for lack of jurisdiction.

The act requires that the special counsel review alleged violations of laws, rules, or regulations; mismanagement; gross waste of funds; abuse of authority; or a substantial and specific danger to public health and safety. If the OSC determines that there is a likelihood of a violation, the special counsel may order that an investigation be made and a written report be forwarded to the agency head, Congress, or to the special counsel within 60 days. If an investigation is not warranted, the head of the agency is still required to notify the special counsel in writing within 60 days of any action taken or to be taken, stating when such action will be completed. The employee making the allegation must also be notified.

In addition to initiating agency investigations, the special counsel also has the responsibility to protect those employees who disclose information concerning agency wrong-doing. If there are reasonable grounds to believe that employer retaliation has occurred, the special counsel can request the MSPB to stay the practice and can bring disci-plinary actions against those who take reprisals against government employees.

The first test of free speech under the act came in August 1979. The issue was whether the Justice Department was justified or punitive in transferring four federal marshals from Atlanta to Florida and Texas. The Justice Department said that the men were troublemakers who tried to disrupt the service and then cover their shortcomings. The Office of Special Counsel and the marshals claimed the trans-fers were in reprisal for their charges that top officials in Atlanta were sometimes incompetent, racist, and permitted improper work conditions.

In late 1979 the three member MSPB upheld the transfer of three deputies.[74] The Government Accountability Pro-ject (GAP), a public interest group, said the MSPB action "sends a signal throughout the bureaucracy: the civil ser-vice reform act will do little to counter the traditional pattern of retaliation against those who fight government misconduct."[75]

The OSC also received criticism from GAP in late 1979. GAP believed that their proposed regulations, which were de-signed to administratively implement the policing responsi-bilities of that office, fell short of the goals of the Civil Service Reform Act.[76] A year later, the Government Accounting Office finished its review of the OSC and identi-fied similar problem areas: 1) case processing delays need to be resolved; 2) there is a need for better communication with whistleblowers; 3) follow-up is needed on agency re-ports; and 4) additional information on special counsel pro-cedures is needed to acquaint employees with the office.[77] Criticisms such as these have led others to call for abolish-ment of the OSC. Representative Patricia Schroeder, one of the founders of the office in 1978, introduced a bill that she says will save the taxpayers millions of dollars a year by closing the office.[78] If it is passed, employees will take their claims directly to the MSPB.

Moreover, GAP plans to study special counsel activities to identify the reasons for inadequate protections in the Civil Service Reform Act. The study is sponsored by the Fund for Constitutional Government, another Washington group.

To resolve these and other problems, the OSC asked Con-gress for more money and additional staff. At present it has a staff of about 95 who handle 225 new cases each month. The Reagan administration budgeted the special counsel for $4.37 million and 120 employment slots in 1982--fewer in both categories than the Office of Management and Budget had proposed under President Carter.

Overall, the act offers a number of advantages over the previous system. First, all employees are guaranteed by statute certain procedural rights in case of an adverse action. Second, appellants can recover attorney fees under certain circumstances.[79] Third, whistleblowers can solicit the assistance of the OSC before or after any retaliatory action.[80] Fourth, protected disclosures now encompass charges which involve no crime. An employee may now complain of mismanagement, gross waste of funds, abuse of authority, or substantial and specific danger to public health and safety.

The Inspectors General

In October 1978 President Carter signed a bill that reorganized the executive branch of the government by establishing Offices of Inspector General within twelve federal departments and agencies. Public Law 95-452 or the "Inspector General Act of 1978", as it is commonly called, consolidated existing auditing and investigative resources to more effectively combat fraud, abuse, waste, and mismanagement in the programs and operations of those departments and agencies.

Recent evidence, brought to light by the press and government officials, showed that fraud, waste, and abuse in federally funded programs had reached epidemic proportions. Several examples will suffice to illustrate the magnitude of the problem: a study done for the Agriculture Department estimated that 8 percent of the $5.5 billion spent in the food stamp program in fiscal year 1977 was erroneously spent--about $440 million.

FBI and General Accounts Office (GAO) investigators found that the General Services Administration (GSA) awarded over $2 million in repairs and alteration contracts which have never been performed.

The House Governmental Operations Committee estimated that at least $375 million may have been wasted on trips of little or no value.[81]

Other proponents of the act cite deficiencies in current federal efforts to combat fraud and waste as reasons for its passage, particularly lack of resources and deficiencies in organizational structure.

Most agencies simply do not have the resources to prevent, much less detect, abuses. For example, the Department of Transportation had only four inspectors to detect fraud in a $6 billion highway program. The Veterans' Administration had one auditor for every $238 million provided by Congress.

Previous federal audit and investigative efforts failed, according to a GAO report, because auditors and investigators reported to, and were under the supervision of, the
very officials whose programs they were supposedly auditing
and investigating.[82] The chief of the Community Services
Administration's Inspection Division testified that he had
been denied permission to investigate allegations of wrongdoing in several cases. In one such case, a later investigation resulted in 22 indictments.

The inspector general concept is based on the premise
that for the audit and investigative capacity to be effective, authority must be vested in an individual reporting
to, and under the supervision of, only the head of the agency. The act not only mandates this, but further states that
the head of the agency may not prohibit, prevent, or limit
the inspector general from undertaking and completing any
audits and investigations that the inspector general deems
necessary.

This legislation creates positions of inspector general
at the Departments of Agriculture, Commerce, Housing and
Urban Development, the Interior, Labor, and Transportation,
and within the Community Services Administration, the National Aeronautics and Space Administration, the Veterans' Administration, the GSA, Environmental Protection Agency, and the
Small Business Administration. Their duties and responsibilities include: 1) providing policy direction for the auditing and investigating activities of the agency; 2) reviewing
existing and proposed legislation and regulations relating
to programs and operations of the agency and to Congress
concerning the enforceability of such legislation and regulation; 3) supervising other activities for the purpose of
promoting economy, efficiency, and effectiveness in the
administration of such programs, or preventing or detecting
fraud and abuse in such programs; 4) coordinating relationships between the agency and other federal agencies, state
and local governmental agencies, and nongovernmental
entities; and 5) keeping the head of the agency and Congress
fully and currently informed concerning fraud and other
serious problems in the operation of programs.[83]

The inspector general system, which is best described
as the consolidation of auditing and investigative responsibilities under a single high-level official, addresses the
major problems confronting current federal efforts to prevent or detect fraud and abuse.

First, the legislation provides a single focal point in
each agency for the effort to deal with fraud in federal
expenditures and programs. Heretofore, the linkage between
investigating and auditing was ineffective due to decentral-
ization of audit units. Some decentralized units were respon-

sible for certain elements of a wide ranging programmatic fraud but were unable to pursue them to their conclusion. Additionally, a single office strengthens cooperation between the agency and the Department of Justice in investigating and prosecuting fraud cases. The Justice Department reports that those agencies that have been the most effective co-partners have been those with viable Offices of Inspector General. [The Departments of Agriculture (1962) and Housing and Urban Development (1972) created the Offices of Inspector General administratively. In 1976 Congress created the first statutory Inspector General at HEW.]

Second, because the inspector general is a presidential appointee, confirmed by the Senate, it is clear that Congress takes the problem and its responsibilities seriously, thereby upgrading the auditing and investigative functions in the executive agencies.

Third, the act gives inspectors general no conflicting policy responsibilities that could divert their attention; their sole responsibility is to coordinate auditing and investigating efforts.

Fourth, the inspectors general have the requisite independence to do an effective job. They are under the general authority of the head of the agency, and not under the supervision of any other official in the agency.

Fifth, because the inspectors general can provide and set forth publicly "best estimates" of current fraud, waste, and abuse in agency programs and operations, Congress and the public derive benefit. Once a problem is identified, management can begin taking corrective steps. Stricter legislation can be adopted.

Inspectors general prepare semi-annual reports in order to disseminate their findings. The reports, initially forwarded to the agency head and later to Congress, are available to the public. They summarize a description of significant problems, abuses, and deficiencies relating to the administration of agency programs; recommendations for corrective action; matters referred to prosecuting authorities and the prosecutions and convictions that have resulted.

In addition to investigating mismanagement, waste, or fraud, the inspectors general may receive and investigate complaints or information from an agency employee concerning abuse of authority or a substantial and specific danger to public health and safety. Moreover, the Civil Service Reform Act of 1978 requires that if a complaint is brought to the attention of the special counsel, he or she should refer the complaint to the agency head for investigation. Consequently, the inspectors general may receive not only complaints from employees but also those that come indirectly from the special counsel via the agency head. Both the Inspector General Act and the Civil Service Reform Act protect the complaining employee by stipulating that the inspector general and special counsel may not disclose the complainant's identity unless they determine that such disclosure is unavoidable during the course of the investigation. Furthermore, no employee is to suffer retaliation as a result of making a complaint or disclosing information to these government officials.

CONCLUSION

Increasingly, courts are being called upon to provide a remedy for discharged employees. As a result there is a growing body of case law that allows private at-will employees to sue their former employers. These exceptions to the employment-at-will doctrine are based upon considerations of public policy. But to date, there are only 13 recognized exceptions; 16 states are reconsidering the doctrine; and 23 states still honor the common law.[84]

Public employees who blow the whistle on their employers cite as support their concern for the public's welfare and their duty to protect societal interests. However, in reaching a decision, the courts have struck an uneasy balance between the employee's First Amendment right to freedom of speech and the efficient operation of government agencies. Thus, public employees' First Amendment rights are vague and vary from court to court, depending on the balance struck. The First Amendment right to petition offers protection if the employee's disclosure is made to an agency superior whom the employee believes can redress the matter, and if the statement is not knowingly false. Procedural protections--constitutional and statutory--also limit an employer's abusive discharge power.

Whether in the public or private sector, whistleblowing employees receive a limited type of protection from federal anti-reprisal provisions. Although they are a step in the right direction and a welcome departure from the employment at will doctrine, these provisions are deficient in several areas. Possible remedies would include extending the filing period to at least 60 days; reinstating the employee pending final disposition of the case if the regulatory agency finds that the complaint was not frivolously brought; allowing a successful complainant to recover the costs of litigation, including attorney fees; and if unsuccessful, allowing a complainant to appeal the decision to a United States court of appeals.

State statutes, also designed to insulate employees from employer retribution, have multiplied in the past few years. At least five states have now enacted such whistleblowing legislation, but it is too early to determine its effectiveness.

Since the 1978 passage of the reform legislation, attention has focused on its effectiveness. Some have severely criticized the MSPB and the OSC, while others have gone further by calling for the abolishment of the OSC. Inspectors general have not escaped public scrutiny, either. They, too, have been accused of being ineffective

In sum although the legislation offers several advantages over the old civil service system as outlined in the preceding discussion, it is clear that agencies can still retaliate against whistleblowing employees. The employee is simply denied promotions and salary increases or given an unsatisfactory performance appraisal. These new federal laws, however, have created legislative protections that were not previously available to whistleblowing employees.

NOTES

1. See, for example, Norman Bowie. "Blowing the Whistle and Other 'Why Be Moral Questions?'", in Business Ethics (Englewood Cliffs, NJ: Prentice-Hall, 1982), pp. 138-149.
2. S. Prakash Sethi, "Allied Chemical and the Kepone Controversy: Responsibility of Corporations and Executives For Damage to Workers' Health and Environmental Safety Arising Out of Improper and Illegal Toxic Waste Disposal." Unpublished paper, Center For Research In Business and Social Policy, The University of Texas at Dallas, 1980.
3. Two of the earliest statements of the employment-at-will doctrine are those of the Tennessee Supreme Court in Payne vs. Western & Atlantic R.R. Co., 81 Tenn. 507 (1884), overruled on other grounds; and Hutton vs. Watters, 132 Tenn. 527, 179 S.W. 134 (1915). For a detailed historical description of the development of the employment-at-will doctrine, see Note, "Implied Contractual Rights to Job Security," Stanford Law Review 26 (1974): 335, 338-340.
4. Lawrence Blades, "Employment At Will vs. Individual Freedom: On Limiting the Abusive Exercise of Employer Power," Columbia Law Review 67 (1967): 1405-1435.
5. 208 U.S. 161 (1908).
6 Blades "Employment at Will", p. 1416.

7. "Job Security," Stanford Law Review, p. 342.
8. For a review of the constitutional protection of the employment interest, see Cornelius J. Peck, "Unjust Discharges From Employment: A Necessary Change in the Law," Ohio State Law Journal 40 (1979): 1-49.
9. 344 P.2d 25 (1959).
10. Id. at 27.
11. Id. at 28.
12. John Conway, "Protecting The Private Sector At Will Employee Who 'Blows the Whistle': A Cause of Action Based Upon Determinants of Public Policy," Wisconsin Law Review 77 (1977): 777-812.
13. Id. at 789. See Framptom vs. Central Indiana Gas Co., 297 N.E.2d 425 (1973) and Sventko vs. Kroger Co., 245 N.W.2d 151 (1976), which both exemplify this approach.
14. See Petermann, supra note 9, which serves well as an example of the implication of both a right and a remedy.
15. Courts have responded in either of two ways: by modifying the doctrine of employment at will (Monge vs. Beebe Rubber Co., 316 A.2d 549 [1974]) or by creating a narrowly defined exception based upon a specific public policy (Nees vs. Hocks, 536 P.2d 512 [1975]).
16. 319 A.2d 174 (1974).
17. Id. at 175.
18. Id. at 178.
19. Id. at 180. The court noted that Geary failed to allege a specific intent by the employer to cause harm by the discharge and had failed to allege that the threat of discharge was performed to coerce him into unlawful activity.
20. 400 F. Supp. 1322 (E.D. Mo. 1975), aff'd, 539 F.2d 1126 (18th Cir. 1976).
21. 400 F. Supp. at 1323.
22. Id. at 1324.
23. See Alfred Feliu, "Discharge of Professional Employees: Protecting Against Dismissal For Acts Within a Professional Code of Ethics," Columbia Human Rights Law Review 11 (1980): 149-187. The jurisdictions are Arizona, California, Illinois, Indiana, Kentucky, Massachusetts, Michigan, New Hampshire, New Jersey, Oregon, Pennsylvania, Washington, and West Virginia.
24. Id. at 155.
25. Campbell vs. Ford Industries, 274 Or. 243, 546 P.2d 141 (1976) and Beckett vs. Welton & Associates, 39 Cal. App.3d 815, 114 Cal. Rptr. 531 (1974).
26. Id.
27. Monge vs. Beebe Rubber Co.

28. Pierce vs. Ortho Pharmaceutical Corp., 166 N.J. Super. 335, 338, 399 A.2d 1023, 1024 (1979), cert. granted 81 N.J. 266, 405 A.2d 810 (1979).
29. See Barsky vs. Bd. of Regents, 347 U.S. 442, 451 (1954); Bailey vs. Richardson, 182 F.2d 46, 59 (D.C. Cir. 1950), aff'd by an equally divided Court, 341 U.S. 918 (1951).
30. 155 Mass. 216, 220, 29 N.E. 517 (1892).
31. Id.
32. 391 U.S. 563 (1968).
33. Id. at 568.
34. Id. at 569.
35. See Elrod vs. Burns, 427 U.S. 347, 367 (1976).
36. 376 F.2d 857 (Ct. Cl. 1967).
37. Id. at 867.
38. Id. at 863, citing New York Times Co. vs. Sullivan, 376 U.S. 254, 280 (1964).
39. 5 U.S.C. Section 7102 (1970).
40. 5 U.S.C. Sections 7501(a), 7512(a) (1970).
41. U.S. Const. amend. V; id. amend. XIV, Section 1. See the companion cases of Board of Regents vs. Roth, 408 U.S. 564 (1972) and Perry vs. Sindermann, 408 U.S. 593 (1972). These cases provide the basis for the definitions of liberty and property to be applied in considering a due process claim.
42. 467 F.2d 755 (D.C. Cir. 1972).
43. Id. at 762.
44. 5 U.S.C. Sections 7501(a), 7512(a) (1970).
45. 5 U.S.C. Sections 7501(b), 7512(b) (1970).
46. Alaska Stat. Section 14.20.180(b)(1) (1971) (public hearing upon employee's request); Mass. Ann. Laws ch. 31, Section 43(b) (1973) (public hearing upon request of either party); N.J. Stat. Ann. 11:15-5 (1960) (investigation, inquiry or hearing shall be open to the public); Pa. Stat. Ann. Title 71 Section 741.951 (Supp. 1975) (public hearing).
47. Alaska Stat. Section 1420.180(c) (1971); Ill. Ann. Stat. ch. 24, Section 10-1-18 (Smith-Hurd Supp. 1974); Mass. Ann. Laws ch. 31, Section 43(a); New York Civ. Serv. Laws Section 75 (McKinney 1973).
48. See, for example, Clyde W. Summers, "Individual Protection Against Unjust Dismissal: Time For A Statute," Virginia Law Review 62 (1976), 481-532.
49. 29 U.S.C. Sections 151-187 (1979).
50. 29 U.S.C. Section 157 (1973).
51. 4 Lab. Rel. Rep. (BNA) 1:42 (January 1979).
52. 42 U.S.C. Section 2000e-2 (1978).
53. 29 U.S.C. Sections 621-634 (1976).
54. 8A Lab. Rel. Rep. (BNA) 451:1011-105 (April 1978).

55. 29 U.S.C. Sections 651-678 (1976). For an analysis of the Act, see Lewis Solomon and Terry Garcia, "Protecting The Corporate Whistleblower Under Federal Anti-Reprisal Statutes," Journal of Corporation Law, 5 (1980): 275-297.

56. 30 U.S.C. Sections 801-960 (1976); amended by Federal Mine Safety And Health Act of 1977, Section 102(a), 30 U.S.C. 801 (Supp. I 1977).

57. 33 U.S.C. Section 901 (1976).

58. 42 U.S.C. Sections 2011-2296 (1976).

59. 33 U.S.C. Section 1251 (1976) (amended 1977).

60. 42 U.S.C. Section 330F (1976).

61. 42 U.S.C. Section 6901 (1976).

62. Occupational Safety and Health Act, Section 10(a), 29 U.S.C. Section 659(a) (1976).

63. 42 U.S.C. Section 7401 (1976).

64. 30 U.S.C. Section 1201 (Supp. I 1977).

65. Of the statutes mentioned, only the Federal Mine and Safety and Health Act allows the individual sixty days within which to file a complaint.

66. 29 U.S.C. Section 660(c)(2) (1976).

67. 4 Lab. Rel. Rep. (BNA) 1:45 (January 1979).

68. Id. at 1:42.

69. Id. at 1:42-43.

70. For example, Conn. Gen. Stat. Ann. 48-61DD(a) (1979), applies to public employees only; Md. Ann. Code Art. 64 Section 12 (1980) applies to public employees only; Louisiana St. Labor Laws 28 Section 1074.1(2) (1981), apply to both public and private employees; Mich. Code Laws Ann. 15.361 (1980), applies to both public and private employees; and Cal. Labor Code Section 432.2 and Cal. Penal Code Section 637.3 (1979), applies only to employees who testify before a joint legislative committee.

71. P.L. 95-454 (1978).

72. General Accounting Office, The Office of Special Counsel Can Improve Its Management of Whistleblower Cases (Washington, D.C.: Government Printing Office, 1980), Appendix I, p.1.

73. Keith Sinzinger, "Union, GAP Enter Fight Over Special Counsel," Federal Times, October 20, 1980.

74. Frazier.

75. Louis Clark and Thomas Devine, "To Protect the Whistleblowers," The Washington Star, May 6, 1980.

76. Inderit Badhwar, "Merit System Policeman Accused of Copping Out," Federal Times, October 8, 1979.

77. General Accounting Office, Management of Whistleblowing.

78. Sinzinger, Keith, "He Welcomes Investigation." Federal Times, May 31, 1982, p. 2.
79. 5 U.S.C.A. Section 7701(g) (West Supp. 1979).
80. 5 U.S.C.A. Section 1206 (a)(1) (West Supp. 1979).
81. U.S. Congress, Senate, Committee on Governmental Affairs, Establishment of Offices of Inspector General and Auditor General in Certain Executive Departments and Agencies. 95th Congress, 2nd Session, 1978.
82. U.S. Congress, Establishment of Offices.
83. P.L. 95-452.
84. See Alfred G. Feliu, "Loyalty, the Employment Relationship and the Law." Paper read at the conference on Conflicting Loyalties in the Workplace, April 2, 1982, Bentley College, Waltham, MA, p. 8.

EIGHT
A STRATEGIC
ANALYSIS

An employee, after much deliberation, may decide to go public with information about his or her organization's wrongdoing. Once the decision is made, he or she must choose among a number of options or strategies. Each has advantages and disadvantages that vary with the circumstances.

One strategy is to enlist the support of community action groups; a sympathetic community leader can offer the resources of his group, [1] and through them bring pressure to bear on businesses or bureaucracies in that locale. Or one may seek to publicize one's case and cause through the media:[2] an aggressive reporter can secure the attention of a broad and diffuse public. Professional societies are a third alternative.[3] To appeal to them is to appeal to one's peers, where in addition to a sympathetic hearing, one can hope for expert advice. Fourth, employees in the federal government can go to the inspector general[4] where a formal or informal federal investigation may take place. A fifth option is to sue, to go to court;[5] this is one official channel of redress that can bring legal pressure to bear on an organization. As a sixth strategy, one can go to the Congress or the Senate;[6] if the issue is national in scope, an appropriate committee can hold a hearing to investigate allegations and determine the facts.

Occasionally the dissident is able to voice his or her concerns within the organization, thereby obviating any need to go public. Consultation and grievance procedures often accommodate dissenting views[7].

Whether an employee seeks redress internally through established channels, circumvents internal channels by going to the top, or goes outside the organization, he or she is wise to formulate a clear plan. In this chapter we shall identify various strategies and try to determine what makes one more appropriate than others and hence more likely to succeed.

One can succeed or fail as a whistleblower in different ways. Accordingly, the first section defines three notions of success. Each of these depends on a different perspective --the objective, personal, and social. The second section identifies five factors that affect success--the issue, organizational characteristics, organizational role, individual traits, and the historical context. The third section appraises the likelihood that a particular strategy will succeed in terms of these five factors, using concrete examples so that the reader can better understand their use. The fourth section concludes with some lessons to be learned [8].

THE CONCEPT OF SUCCESS

Before we can determine whether a whistleblower has succeeded or failed, we need to know what success is.[9] In different contexts the word can have different meanings. It depends in part on how one looks at success. At least three different perspectives can be adopted that of a disinterested onlooker; that of the individual; and that of the courts.

Objective Success

For the whistleblower to be successful, some change must occur in response to his or her concerns. Clearly, if no change whatsoever occurs, then in no sense can the whistleblower be called a success. But what kind of change is necessary, and how much is required?

The change may be appraised according to one or more of the following five criteria:

1. the wrongdoing was stopped or prevented;
2. the concerns were shown to be unfounded;
3. the policy was changed;

4. the organization was prosecuted or convicted;
5. individuals were able to avoid becoming victims
of the wrongdoing.

If the wrongdoing the whistleblower protests ceases,
then he or she is a success.

These same criteria can be stated somewhat differently.[10] Dissent is successful if one raises his or her
voice and gets action. If one literally blows a whistle, he
or she must blow loudly enough to be heard. Once blown,
others must heed its message and act accordingly--by reducing the probability of similar wrongs in the future, by
compensating victims of past wrongs, by preventing or lessen-
ing the risk of future wrongs, or by disproving the dissident's hypothesis.

Personal Success

This definition is subjective and refers to the whistleblower's personal, internal point of view. It connotes a
sense of winning, a personal triumph. Did he or she achieve
what he or she had in mind? One can only answer this question if one is aware of the dissident's intentions--to be
heard, to right a wrong, to punish the perceived wrongdoer.

Social Success

One can achieve success if one's efforts are vindicated
in the eyes of others. If one's friends, family, co-workers,
colleagues, or a community group praise one's efforts, or
recognize the importance of the concerns raised, then in
this third sense one has succeeded. This vindication can
come through any number of institutions including community
groups, Congress, professional associations, and the media.

One familiar social organization is the courts. The
law, by its nature, clearly states principles and issues.
One can win or lose (or win one point and lose another).
Legal success occurs when a party to an action sues and is
awarded damages or some legal form of relief. But law is in
a constant state of flux. At any particular point it represents a link in a chain. Even though a dissident may not
have been awarded damages or compensated in some other way,
he or she may have been instrumental in establishing new
standards (or precedents) for future cases. An example may
clarify this point[11]. The court denied damages to a plaintiff. Technically, she lost her action. But, one judge, in
his dissenting opinion, stated that because the plaintiff
was upholding her professional standards, the employment-

at-will doctrine[12] should not have applied. This opinion is on permanent public record. Future similar cases may cite it in support of other actions--all the links are connected.

FACTORS IN SELECTING A STRATEGY

Given that the employee has arrived at the point of action--where does he or she go? Who will help? An employee may contact the media, the courts, a professional society, Congress, the inspectors general, community action groups, consultants, or appeal through grievance procedures. Most likely he or she will rely on only one strategy. What criteria will determine which mechanism should be used or, whether or not it will be appropriate and successful?

The Whistleblower's Perspective

Although numerous options may be available to the dissident, he or she may not be aware of all of them. Those less involved may see several distinct alternatives, each with advantages and disadvantages, but prospective whistleblowers may not. They may be so caught up in their own problems-- focused on the corporate wrongdoing and its failure to act constructively. Emotionally, they may feel trapped and ineffective--conscious of the problem and the remedy but unaware of the link between the two. So, we should keep in mind that these employees may be quite uninformed and consequently ignorant of some of the options.

Automatic Exclusion

From the beginning some channels will probably be barred. Jurisdiction and scope of authority limit the uses of some mechanisms. For instance local community groups have no authority over corporate policy in Washington. The inspectors general, having jurisdiction over government agencies only, cannot investigate alleged abuse by private corporations.

The Issue

The subject at issue may shape the whistleblower's tactics. For instance local environmental concerns are tailor made for local environmental action groups. Technical engineering or scientific concerns are best understood by fellow professionals--consultants or professional groups.

The misappropriation of government monies should be brought to the the attention of those (voters) who will pressure government officials to remedy the situation--perhaps through the media.

Organizational Characteristics [13]

Organizations are tall or flat (hierarchal or layered), have a wide or narrow span of authority, are centralized or decentralized, are old or young. Some organizational cultures are marked by a high degree of control and autocratic decision making while others are known for their participative style and open channels of communication. All of these factors help determine what procedures (or lack of them) are available to resolve disputes.

One's Organizational Role

The whistleblower usually occupies a diffuse and general role. He or she has access to information regarding the attainment of organizational goals and is somewhat insulated from day to day activities. His or her role, although ambiguous, often permits substantial discretion and responsibility.

Professional roles may lend themselves to employing a particular strategy. For instance one who functions as a liaison or public informant may be in regular contact with the press. Even before assuming a dissenting position, this person is familiar with the mechanism. One who is a political appointee knows one's way around politicians and easily maneuvers in these circles. Of course the converse can also be true. One who is familiar with an outside organization (like the FDA) may consciously avoid it when blowing the whistle, believing it to be incompetent. A symbiotic relationship may arise between a scientist and an environmental group--exchanging information for lobbying. If a time comes when the scientist needs support for his or her dissenting views he or she might ask "friends" for help.

Individual Traits

The dissident's personality may predispose him or her to prefer one strategy over another. A shy, unobtrusive person prefers not to make a public appearance. Perhaps this person will speak to the public through someone else (a witness, perhaps). This kind of person prefers to remain in the background. On the other hand those with a dramatic flair or propensity toward public relations are at home on center stage. The media suits these types. Some people avoid authority figures--like the courts and Congress. Others gravitate toward them. Some trust their peers and are likely to defer to their professional association. Some, who uphold fairness, will turn to an impartial arbiter--like the court.

Historical Context

Trends, fads, and fluctuating political atmosphere affect not only whether or not the public is sympathetic to the cause but also which medium will be most effective in getting action.

For example, antinuclear groups were barely visible 15 years ago. But they have gained national recognition within the past ten years. The consumer movement of the past decade has accounted for new regulatory and investigative agencies (like the Inspectors General Office) and pro-consumer legislation. Bureaucracy is rapidly becoming a dirty word as evidenced by modification of the Employment at Will Doctrine and recent protective legislation for whistleblowers (occupational health and safety legislation and environmental laws).

The individual involved, his or her organization and professional role, the issue, and the mechanism he or she employs to go public combine in a unique mix which determines his success. The following section discusses each strategy in relation to this mix.

We will begin with an internal strategy--consultations. The remaining strategies will be discussed in order of their distance from the organization. Community groups and the media are one step away from the organization. One can "leak" information to these people quietly (and anonymously) from inside their organizations. The professional association can assume a low profile. It tends to be a nonthreatening entity. Whereas once the inspector general has been contacted, a formal authoritative investigation is undergone. Both the courts and Congress wield substantial power and are highly visible. Third parties are brought into the picture (for example, lawyers, members of congress, and expert witnesses); formal public proceedings are held; and accompanying publicity broadcasts the findings.

ANALYZING THE OPTIONS

Internal Avenues

Efforts to resolve conflicts within the organization sometimes succeed. Even if the dissident must ultimately seek outside assistance, at least his or her internal efforts have strengthened the case. A legal analog to "work things out inside first" is known as the "exhaustion of remedies" principle by which a potential litigant seeks relief from a responsible government agency before he or she can be heard in court. The dissident who attempts to persuade management must present evidence of his or her claim. The employer is given a chance to respond. By the time the employee finally goes public, he or she has probably constructed a well-supported case. It is very unlikely that the employee will be accused of being disloyal or unfair.

On the other hand some concerns, by their nature, require immediate action; risking delay is dangerous. For instance, a nuclear leak, unsafe scaffolding, or poisonous sewage will cause irreversible damage should no immediate action be taken. If swift authoritative enforcement is required, then blowing the whistle is in order.

One method of handling technical disputes is through consultation. Our discussion will focus on a scientific research laboratory that emphasizes good communication through informal and formal consultations with colleagues, administrators, and outside experts.

The laboratory developed and tested its informal mechanism for resolving conflict over its 25-year history. Basically, it has one client, the government, and rarely deals with other organizations (and their perspectives and values). One-third of the staff hold advanced degrees, mostly in the sciences--including management. Scientific standards and norms are generally accepted.

Professional roles are flexible. Scientists assume a great deal of responsibility that is marked by autonomy and discretion.[14] They respect and defer to each other's judgment as proven scientists.

Dissent is not uncommon. But by the time all internal channels have been exhausted (sometimes an eternity) the matter has usually been resolved.

Clearly, consultation at the laboratory is a successful method of resolving conflict--by both objective and subjective definitions. Voices are loud and clear. Concerns are shown to be founded or unfounded and policy is affected accordingly. Personally, the dissident has spoken, has been listened to, and is satisfied enough that he or she accepts the final decision.

External Mechanisms

Perhaps the employee is unable or unwilling to resolve the conflict internally. He or she is then confronted with the prospect of blowing the whistle. Will he be fired . . . hated . . . depressed or ostracized? What are his or her chances of winning and preventing the damage or harm? He or she may be concerned with remaining anonymous. How?

Whatever the considerations, the plan of action is crucial to the outcome. The following section will discuss several mechanisms in relation to the employee's strategy.

Community Groups

The regional director for a government environmental agency accused his employer of disregarding serious environmental threats connected with the storage of chemical waste below ground. He attempted to block the planned disposal of the waste by contacting a community action group who shared his concerns. He leaked information to the group who, in turn, applied pressure on the agency to hold a public hearing (at which members of the group testified). The waste was subsequently buried in another state--merely displacing the problem. As a result of the director's strict environmental stance, he was demoted and later resigned.

He was a respected--but unpopular--engineer with 35 years of experience. His colleagues and superiors accused him of being scrappy and difficult. But the local community groups considered him a dedicated friend--both were on the same side of the fence.

Did he successfully blow the whistle? No. The chemicals were still improperly disposed of. Nothing changed.

His concerns were not heeded, and policy remained the same. He considered himself defeated and eventually resigned.

The Media

A wildlife pathologist for an environmental agency charged his employer with contributing to the state's environmental problems by allowing industry to discharge large amounts of chemical waste into rivers and streams. He sent more than 100 memoranda warning of the problem to various members of the agency over a five-year period. Getting no action, he became thoroughly disgruntled and decided to go public by informing local reporters. Management disapproved and severely limited his resources--cutting back his staff and budget. As a result of his actions, the department halted the dumping of certain toxic chemicals into the rivers.

What did the media offer? First, because the pathologist enjoyed a great deal of autonomy, both as a professional and as a civil servant, press coverage did not threaten his livelihood. Second, the media trusted the accuracy of his reports because he had a track record of sound and well-documented scientific judgment. He also had easy access to material data that increased his value as an informant. Third, the head office was extremely sensitive to political pressure. Though he personally had no political savvy, he could effectively use the media to bear down on the administration. Fourth, he enjoyed the accompanying publicity and recognition. Fifth, the media is engaging--both entertaining and colorful. It precisely suits the pathologist's aim. Seventh, it can release information at an appropriate moment--when the audience is ripe.

The pathologist was indeed successful in preventing wrongdoing, substantiating his claim, causing policy to change, and preventing people from becoming victimized. He also accomplished his intentions--to protect the environment.

Professional Associations

A computer scientist, employed by a hospital, feared that the intended installation of a new patient computer billing system would overload the mainframe and cause the existing patient monitoring system to fail at a crucial moment. The patient monitoring system informed the medical staff when a patient's vital signs became critical so that immediate medical attention could be given to the critically ill patient. After voicing her concern, the scientist was fired for insubordination. A committee of her professional association investigated her allegations and found that her attempt to stop the installation was professionally justified by the code of ethics.

What did the professional association offer? First, one of its committees was established to investigate alleged harm done to its members as a result of their adherence to the professional code. If the committee made a decision to support a member, it pressured the industry by publishing the wrongdoing (including names)--sort of a wrist slapping. Depending on the size and strength of the professional organization, the industry may or may not pay attention. For instance, the AMA wields tremendous power, whereas smaller associations are barely even recognized.

Second, some issues are highly technical and can only be thoroughly understood and evaluated by others who possess the requisite knowledge--colleagues, professionals, and specialists. When an employee does not work with fellow experts, he or she may seek the opinions and support of a reference group, in this case, a professional organization.

Third, morally founded objections can sometimes be justified by citing sections of one's code of ethics. But, while the code may support an employee's actions, it does not always have the power of enforcement. Often it functions more as a mouthpiece than as a whip.

Fourth, professional ethics is a growing field. Investigative committees are becoming a common feature of these associations. In the case at hand, the committee had recently been formed and was anxious to test its effectiveness and gain a reputation in the industry.

Was the computer scientist successful? Yes. The patient billing system was never installed. Consequently, no one was hurt, and potential wrongdoing was prevented. Even though she was personally tormented throughout the episode, she considered herself triumphant.

The Inspector General

One of our cases involved an engineer for a major government construction project. He accused his department of overlooking numerous structural safety hazards. Unable to resolve the matter internally, he contacted the inspector general who ordered a full scale investigation that eventually substantiated most of the engineer's charges.

The Inspector General Act of 1978 (Public Law 95-452) was established in response to these inadequacies. It provides for the consolidation of auditing and investigative responsibilities, under a single, high-level official. The recently formed agency investigates accusations of fraud, abuse, waste, and mismanagement in 12 federal departments (an inspector general is appointed to each).

Informing the inspector general offers several benefits to those who use this avenue. First, the creation of the position of inspector general has established a focal point in each agency to deal with fraud. Second, the inspector general is a presidential appointment which Congress takes seriously. Third, the inspector general's sole responsibility is the coordination of audits and investigations--a clear objective without conflicts. Fourth, the position of inspector general is under the sole authority of the head of the agency--allowing independent judgment and autonomy.

Was he successful? Yes. Resources were mobilized and the construction faults were corrected, thereby diminishing risk and saving potential victims. No one was hurt. And most of the engineer's claims were corroborated.

The Courts

A research scientist was concerned that her employer, a pharmaceutical company, not market what she considered to be a dangerous drug. After her internal efforts failed, she resigned and later sued the company for damages, reasoning that she had been constructively discharged.

What did the court offer? First, it provided a structured forum for dispute. Each side was given an opportunity to support its claims. Second, it neither favored nor disfavored either side. As an impartial arbiter, it would resolve the matter fairly. Third, the court and its accompanying publicity informs not only those present but also the public--the medical and legal communities, the consumers, the industry, and the government. Information is broadly disseminated. Fourth, the final decision is binding and enforceable. After it reaches the final level of appeal, no other government body can override its decision (with the exception of, perhaps, a presidential pardon). Fifth, the legal system relies on the principle of stare decisis--precedent. Any similar case before it can be cited as authority.

Was the scientist successful? In an objective sense she was. Of Dr. Deborah Johnson's five criteria, three were clearly satisfied. The drug was never marketed. Therefore, wrongdoing was prevented. The company withdrew its plans to sell it--a policy change. People did not consume it--no one was victimized.

In a personal sense she won. Although damages were denied, she believed that her primary concern was satisfied--the matter was aired impartially and publicly. The coverage of the case informed many people, especially doctors, who might otherwise have remained uninformed and unconcerned.

Legally, she was not successful. She lost the suit for damages. But, as a consequence of her action, one judge, in his dissenting opinion stated that the employment-at-will doctrine should not have applied to her situation. This public record is available to any and all who seek similar relief in the future. It may be just the beginning of a trend to modify the law.

Congress

The case that follows took place in the early years of the antinuclear movement. At that time the proponents of the industry far outweighed its opponents. The prospect of abundant and inexpensive fuel in a time of diminishing resources was very attractive. A systems engineer charged the entire nuclear industry with seriously threatening the environment. His case was heard at a Senate subcommittee hearing.

Clearly, Congress possesses power on a national level that can be used to tremendous effect. But the willingness of congressional members to step forward without the explicit support of their constituencies is often abated by political considerations--lost votes and friends. Once a movement is clearly established and supported by many followers, it becomes safe for a politician to support the cause. But before that time a politician is risking his or her political career by initiating unsupported action.

Was the engineer successful? No. The industry barely shuddered. Congress did not investigate the matter, nor did it take any action. The criticisms were so broad that even an investigation would have been a tremendous undertaking--especially on behalf of one person. One lost vote was not worth fretting over.

Even in the engineer's own judgment he failed. He had hoped to launch a formal investigation of the industry. Instead, he lost his job, career, and friends.

Later, after the movement was well under way, and public concern was apparent, some congressional members began heeding the warnings and were persuaded to act.

STRATEGIC LESSONS

The dissident should carefully consider some important points before adopting a strategy. As we have seen, each situation is unique and should be assessed individually. But, based on the experiences of others, we can make some suggestions.

Consider the Costs

Be careful. Your situation may require a heavy investment--in a lost job, career, friends, colleagues, sleep, and fortunes. Recognize that you are gambling and the odds are against you. Pursue the plan of action that will diminish the costs, if possible.

Seek Support

Are there any laws, regulations, codes of ethics, special interest groups, or documented job descriptions that will support your cause? If so, clearly identify them and plan a strategy that will include them. For instance the courts may be most effective if your concerns are founded in statutes. A regulatory agency can enforce a breach of regulations. Professional codes of ethics usually dedicate one's allegiance to the public good. If your employer forced you to violate these ethical standards perhaps you should consult your professional association.

Define the Issue

What is the nature of the issue--political, scientific, administrative? How broad a scope does it cover? Will it affect only a few people in a particular field, or is it of national concern? Who cares--doctors, politicians, women, fishermen? Does anyone oppose you--administrators, the industry? Is it a complex problem or one that can be communicated in simple terms?

In answering these questions you will form a plan and help identify the most appropriate strategy. For instance a local environmental safety issue might best be addressed by a community action group.

Weigh the Importance

To determine how important the issue is, ask yourself: "If nothing were to be done about it, what would happen?" The greater the potential harm that would result if you did nothing, the more reason you should speak out.

Research the Options

Carefully consider the alternative mechanisms. You will increase your chances of winning by choosing a strategy that best suits the situation.

Verify Your Information

The burden of proof is yours. To strengthen your position, rely on documentation--lab reports, memoranda, expert opinions, or photographs.

NOTES

1. See F. Elliston, J. Keenan, P. Lockhart, and J. van Schaick, "Fighting a State Bureaucracy Through Community Groups," in Whistleblowing: Managing Dissent in the Workplace (New York: Praeger, 1984), pp. 45-58.
2. See "Pesticides and the Press," in Whistleblowing: Managing Dissent in the Workplace (New York: Praeger, 1984), pp. 59-70.
3. See "Politics, Protest, and the Professional Society," in Whistleblowing: Managing Dissent in the Workplace (New York: Praeger, 1984), pp. 71-82.
4. See "Life, Safety, and Inspector General," in Whistleblowing: Managing Dissent in the Workplace (New York: Praeger, 1984), pp. 85-99.
5. See "The Courts: The Physician vs The Drug Company," in Whistleblowing: Managing Dissent in the Workplace (New York: Praeger, 1984), pp. 103-119.
6. See "The Congress and Nuclear Dissent," in Whistleblowing: Managing Dissent in the Workplace (New York: Praeger, 1984), pp. 121-138.
7. See "Consultants and Consultation," in Whistleblowing: Managing Dissent in the Workplace (New York: Praeger, 1984), pp. 27-43.
8. For more lessons, see R. Nader, P. Petkas, and K. Blackwell, eds., "To Blow the Whistle," in Whistle Blowing (New York: Grossman, 1972), pp. 226-243.
9. See Chapter One (this volume), pp. 3-23.
10. See Chapter One (this volume), especially pp. 17-19.
11. Pierce vs. Ortho Pharmaceutical Corp., 166 N.J. Super. 335, 338, 399 A.2d 1023, 1024 (1979), cert. granted 81 N.J. 266, 405 A.2d 810 (1979).
12. See Chapter Seven (this volume) for a discussion of the employment-at-will doctrine and Lawrence Blades, "Employment At Will vs. Individual Freedom: On Limiting the Abusive Exercise of Employer Power," Columbia Law Review 67 (1967): 1405-1435.
13. More is said about organizational characteristics and roles in Chapter Two (this volume).
14. Characteristics of scientists are remarked upon in C.G. Smith, "Consultation and Decision Processes in a Research Laboratory," Administrative Science Quarterly 15 (1970): 203-215 and A.W. Gouldner, "Cosmopolitans versus Locals," Administrative Science Quarterly 2 (Dec. 1957): 282-292.

PART FOUR
ETHICAL
ANALYSES

NINE
CIVIL DISOBEDIENCE AND WHISTLEBLOWING

APPRAISING FORMS OF DISSENT

When, if ever, is an employee morally justified in blowing the whistle on his or her employer? This question is a difficult one to answer definitively and finally. Indeed, it is difficult to know where to begin to look for an answer.

In the Republic, Plato posed the question of justice—what is it, and why should each of us choose it? He too found it a difficult question, but he found a way to ease his labors. He thought he could look for justice "writ large" in the state where it is easier to see.[1] So, too, we may find an answer to our question if we look to a highly visible analogue in the state—civil disobedience.

Large organizations, like governments, demand loyalty from their members. Whether they are private governments as Perucci claims or not,[2] they expect their rules regulating corporate conduct will be followed,[3] and this expectation is usually met. But occasionally their members decide for moral reasons to breach this loyalty, to refuse the demands of fealty in the name of justice or the social good. As a form of dissent against the powerful actions of others, whistleblowing invites comparison to political dissent in the form of civil disobedience. The comparison will not only serve to clarify its meaning but provide a means for deepening our understanding and sharpening our assessment of whistleblowing.

THE CONCEPT OF CIVIL DISOBEDIENCE

Civil disobedience can be defined in different ways.[4] A comparatively non-controversial definition would include the following three elements. First, one's action must be illegal; one cannot commit an act of civil disobedience without breaking the law. The difficulty here is not strategic but conceptual; a legal act by definition would never qualify as disobedience. Second, one's act must be undertaken for a moral reason; illegal actions motivated by self-interest qualify simply as crimes, not civil disobedience. Third, one's action must be undertaken for the purpose of changing a law one finds morally objectionable--typically by drawing attention to it in breaking it.

According to some, for an action to count as an instance of civil disobedience, three further conditions must be satisfied. First, it must be non-violent since the use of raw power against another without his or her consent is uncivilized. Second, it must be direct; the law that is broken must be the law to which one objects. Thus, breaking one regulation by burning your draft card to protest another government practice such as the war in Vietnam would not count. And third, the person who engages in civil disobedience must demonstrate respect for the rule of law by accepting the punishment. To evade it is to call one's motives into question and thereby disqualify one's actions as civil disobedience.

But I believe these last three conditions are strategical, not conceptual, and reflect not so much what whistleblowing is but the conditions under which it is judged to be justified. The strategies adopted by civil disobedients may affect our moral appraisal of their actions, but they should not cloud our identification of them as civil disobedience.

THE TOPOGRAPHY OF DISSENT

Is an act of civil disobedience morally justified? The question has been debated since Socrates.[5] Before attempting an answer, I shall identify some issues that must be resolved. Doing so will indicate how the analogous topic of corporate dissent can be broached.

Alternative Avenues of Dissent

Frequently, critics claim that if civil disobedience is to be justified at all, it can only be as a last resort. To break the law before one has exhausted all other avenues of change is morally reprehensible. This stipulation does not necessarily advocate civil disobedience when all other remedies have failed, but condemns such acts when the alternatives have not been tried. What can be said for or against this last-resort proviso?

On one hand it is the logical consequence of one's obligation to obey the law. If one can avoid breaking the law, one should do so--and the only way to discover whether one can do so is to try the alternatives. All other things being equal, if one can achieve one's objective by legal means, these means should be employed.

On the other side critics point out that things are not always so simple. To write one's member of congress, petition city hall, attend meetings, organize citizens, form political alliances, run for office--these take time and resources that occasionally may not be available. Immediate action is called for, which the political machinery is too slow and cumbersome to provide.

The same issue arises with whistleblowing. Are employees morally obliged to exhaust all internal avenues of change before going public? No doubt some would insist that they should indeed write memos to their superiors, organize their co-workers, contact top management, or go to the board of directors if needed--before they go outside the corporation. But not all would see this emphasis on internal dissent as an absolute.

Nader, for example, comes down on both sides.[6] Because of the contractual relation between an employee and a corporation, like the social contract on which political obligations are based, an employee may be said to have a prima facie obligation to pursue internal mechanisms before bringing outside pressure to bear. Yet this is not always possible.

Some organizations have no means to deal with differences of opinions from within--no ombudsman, grievance system, or open-door policy, at least none that is regularly used and works. Also, pursuing these avenues may be expensive in terms of time and effort, ineffective and slow - delaying the immediate action that is required.[7]

Accordingly, in the case of both political and corporate dissent, one can recognize an initial obligation to try to redress problems from within, but if no mechanisms exist to do so quickly and effectively, one is justified in going outside the corporation.

Public or Anonymous

Dissent may take a variety of forms, from writing letters to testifying before congressional committees. It may also vary along a continuum of publicness. Political dissidents may send unsigned warnings to the executives of the chemical plant threatening to blow up the plant if their illegal practice of dumping pollutants into the water is not halted immediately. Such threats would be less effective if they were signed, and the dissenters' actions would not succeed if they were done publicly in broad daylight.

So too corporate whistleblowers may send unsigned memos to top management informing them of dangerous or illegal practices that need to be curbed or make anonymous telephone calls to investigators.[8] Their anonymity may provide the protection without which they would be unwilling to protest corporate misconduct.[9]

But concealing one's identity has a price. The fact that one will not stand up and be counted makes one's motives suspect. Others may wonder: What do they have to fear that they must hide themselves? Because of this suspicion, integrity becomes questionable. Does the person seek the public good or some private gain? Is this dissident acting in response to the call of conscience or out of spite and contrariness? Such doubts can undermine the effectiveness of dissent. In addition anonymity can impede the flow of information vital to success. Typically, the anonymous dissenter cannot be challenged, cannot respond to challenges, and cannot participate fully in the debate, further curtailing the effectiveness of this form of dissent.

CONFLICTING LOYALTIES

In conceptualizing the phenomenon of dissent, one must recognize that loyalties to different groups come into conflict.[10] The problem is to establish priorities among these, to determine which should take precedence.

In the context of political dissent, the limits of loyalty to one's government are at issue. The Nuremburg Code clearly states that the obligation to obey the law does not override all other obligations.[11] Specifically, it recognizes that individuals have a higher loyalty to the principles of morality.

An analogous point is embodied in the Code of Ethics for United States Government Service approved by the 85th Congress. It states at the outset that any government employee should "put loyalty to the highest moral principles and to country above loyalty to persons, party or Government department." But its failure to elaborate these "highest moral principles" in any detail makes the code dangerously vague, especially combined with the inability of Congress to protect whistleblowers who abide by this provision. And its failure to recognize others to whom one likewise owes loyalty (such as one's family, one's friends, one's God) makes it, ironically, totalitarian.

For example, whistleblowers have generally experienced tremendous personal hardships.[12] What of their obligations to their spouses or to themselves? To mandate self-sacrifice, with no effective safeguards, violates one of the highest moral principles--a sense of justice. [13]

Professionals stand in a variety of social relationships. On the job they have obligations to their immediate co-workers and to their employers. At home they have commitments to their families, their spouses and children. And they have obligations to their friends and even to themselves. Each relationship makes moral demands on the person to consider how much harm is to be done by failure to dissent. DeGeorge usefully distinguishes between permissible and mandatory whistleblowing, as two different thresholds depending on the degree of harm to be done.[14] How are the obligations arising from these factors to be balanced? The view that one relationship--to one's employer--that under all conditions preempts all others is simple-minded and insidious.

More realistically and morally, when these obligations come into conflict, we weigh the seriousness of the particular issue at hand. If it is a matter or responding to wrongdoing by anyone--child, spouse, co-worker--one of our first tasks is to weigh the amount of harm to be done. If it is trivial, we are less obliged to take action. But if a serious harm may be done to a large number of people, then we must seriously weigh protesting it--internally if time permits, externally if that would be more effective.

In addition to the harm, we must also weigh our role and its responsibilities. If it falls within our power and authority, we are more enjoined to action. Even if it does not, we may be obliged to bring it to the attention of those with the responsibility--rather than doing nothing.

A third factor is the strength of the evidence. The more we can document wrongdoing, the stronger the obligation to take action. Mere suspicions or hunches are not sufficient to justify whistleblowing.

Certainly one can dismiss the extreme view that loyalty to one's employer or government overrides all other obligations. But it is more difficult to state the correct view on the limits of this obligation. An analysis of the sources of the duty of fidelity emerges out of an understanding, more or less explicit, between an individual and a larger group. Social contract theorists such as Locke, Hume, and Hobbes regard social and political order as the product of an agreement.[15] In Hobbes each individual surrenders his sovereign power of unmitigated self-seeking to an artificial Leviathan in return for protection of his life and property. Such a contract ends the war of all against all, enabling each to escape the state of nature where one's lot is solitary, poor, nasty, brutish, and short. Though each retains an inalienable right to protect his or her own life, he or she is otherwise obliged to obey the commands of the sovereign. This obligation arises from the covenant of free people and is rooted in the general obligation to keep one's promises.

The contract theory can readily be extended from governments to corporations. When hired, an individual enters into an agreement to serve the interests of his employer, in some more or less defined fashion, in return for certain considerations--wages, job security, holidays, fringe benefits, and so on. As a free agent the employee is bound by the provisions of the contract so long as his or her employer keeps his or her commitments. Typically the contract itself provides for revisions and termination, according to mutually agreed upon procedures.

The social approach has its limitations. According to Hobbes, provided the sovereign maintains law and order, protects my life, limb, and property, I am under an absolute obligation to obey the sovereign's dictates however blatantly "immoral" or "unjustified" they might seem. For the alternative, according to Hobbes, is a return to social and political anarchy which is always worse than the abuses of political power. However, to some, less fearful of chaos, who hold the principles of justice in higher regard, the rule of law is not such an absolute. An unjust law is no law,[16] and one cannot be bound under it to commit injustices.[17] This logic provides one argument to justify acts of disobedience against governments or corporations. If the principles of justice take precedence over the obligation to keep promises, then all covenants are suspended in the face of blatant injustices.

The contractarian theory has its Marxist critics.[18] They insist that such a logic, to be compelling, presupposes that the parties to the contract enter into the negotiations as equals. According to Hobbes this condition is satisfied at a very rudimentary level; each person has an equal power, acting singly or in concert with others, to take another's life. In terms of the power to kill, we are all on the same footing. If it were merely a matter of survival, Hobbes would undoubtedly be complete and compelling.

But if the quality of life takes precedence over quantity, his viewpoint will not suffice. If we are concerned not with living but living the good life (however defined), then the inequalities among people--both natural and acquired--must be taken into account. If I am rich and powerful and you are poor and weak, a contract is simply a mechanism to perpetuate my superiority. If I have the only job you need to earn a living, a contract is a potent weapon for exploitation; I can stipulate that you work long hours at a meager pay, that you make me my coffee, stroke my ego, grant me sexual favors--all as conditions for your employment.[19] And, of course, you can in principle exercise your autonomy and reject these terms. But I can hire another, and you can only suffer the ensuing degradation.

The results of bartering can be fair only if the parties enter into it as free and equal agents. In modern times trade unions and professional societies have helped equalize the balance of power. But in many situations, the job hunter confronts the prospective employer alone, with higher costs to rejecting the contract. Given these inequalities, the demands of loyalty readily serve to dehumanize and degrade others in the name of profit or some other corporate interest.

BREACHING THE LIMITS OF LOYALTY

The above account clarifies the limits of obligation to governments or employers. The results of any contract would be binding only to the extent that the parties enter into it as equals. Conversely, actions that would not be agreed on by equally situated negotiators are not binding. Rawls' methodology and principles of justice provide more content to this statement.[20]

A situation of equality can be approximated if one assumes that one does not know what one's social situation is. Assuming such a veil of ignorance and that each is rational (capable of deliberating about means to freely chosen ends) and self-interested (acts so as to achieve ends that constitute one's personal happiness), Rawls contends we would choose the following three general principles to govern social relations, institutions, and practices. First, one would want to maintain the greatest personal autonomy compatible with a like liberty for all. Second, one would want offices and positions to which differential rewards attach to be open to all on a competitive basis. And third, one would want the differential rewards that attach to these office to be justified on the grounds that they work to the advantage of the least advantaged. These principles, applied to political and corporate dissent, provide a justification for protest.

The actions of civil rights demonstrators find their rationale in the first principle.[21] Blacks were denied the liberties to which whites were entitled—the freedom to eat when they choose, live where they choose, attend school where they choose. The violation of the principle of maximal equal liberty justifies their protests.

Women who protest the sexist policies of management can ground their actions in Rawls' first principle. No company has the right to discriminate among its employees on the basis of race or sex: to fail to promote someone simply because he or she is black or female can never be justified, and every individual has an unqualified right to condemn publicly such racist or sexist practices.

Rawls' second principle provides a basis for protesting collusion. Corporations, both in terms of their collective interests and justice, must keep their offices open to each and all on a fair competitive basis. Racist and sexist bias is one violation of this principle. But so too would any other obstacle to promotion not based on merit and performance. To deny someone an opportunity to advance just because he or she is too old, too tall, divorced (read unstable), or married (likely to move with a husband) is likewise unwarranted. A principle of meritocracy should predominate in corporate ethics.

Finally, according to Rawls' third principle, corporations would have a social commitment.[22] Minimally, they must not exploit the vulnerable, the poor, the unemployed, or the underpaid. Maximally, they should see to it that within society and their company such individuals are well served—not simply not taken advantage of but given every opportunity to advance and prosper. Good citizenship is a requirement not just of individuals but collectivities, and it requires a conscience that is sensitive to the needs of the disadvantaged. Practices that are insensitive to their needs, that disregard or denigrate them, are rightly protested—in either the political or economic arena.

NOTES

This is a revised version of a paper originally published in The Journal of Business Ethics 1 (Spring 1982): 23-28.

1. See The Republic of Plato, tr. Francis M. Cornford (New York: Oxford, 1945), pp. 55ff.
2. Robert Perruci, R.M. Anderson, D. Schendel, and L. Trachman, "Whistle-Blowing: Professional Resistance to Organizational Authority." Paper presented at the Annual Meeting of the American Sociological Association, San Francisco, September 4-8, 1978.
3. The point was made forcefully in "The Corporation," televised by CBS in December 1973. A chief executive officer of Phillips Petroleum, when asked what qualities his company looks for in prospective employees, replied unhesitatingly: "Loyalty."
4. For an excellent collection of materials, see Hugo Bedau, Civil Disobedience: Theory and Practice (New York: Pegasus, 1969). Perhaps the best single analysis by a philosopher is Carl Cohen's Civil Disobedience, Conscience, Tactics and the Law (New York: Columbia University Press, 1971).
5. See Plato's dialogues Apology and Crito.
6. See Nader's Whistle-Blowing (New York: Grossman Publishers, 1972).
7. Alan Westin acknowledges that slowness could under some conditions justify circumventing institutional channels. See his Whistleblowing: Loyalty and Dissent in the Corporation (New York: McGraw, 1980), p. 150.
8. The federal government in the United States has instituted a hotline on which unidentified callers can report wasteful or abusive actions of other employees.
9. For a more thorough moral defense of this practice, see Chapter Ten (this volume), pp. 147-163.
10. There are several philosophical discussions of loyalty. See, for example, Josia Royce, The Philosophy of Loyalty (New York: The Macmillan Co., 1908), pp. 17 ff; John Ladd, "Loyalty," in Encyclopedia of Philosophy, ed. Paul Edwards, vol. 5, p. 97; Andrew Oldenquist, "Loyalty," The Journal of Philosophy 39 (April 1982): 173-193; and Marcia Baron, The Moral Status of Loyalty (Chicago, IL: Center for the Study Ethics in the Professions, 1983).
11. Carl Cohen discusses the application of the Nuremburg judgments in Chapter Eight of his book (opus cit., Note 3). For a cogent discussion of the limits of the loyalty by agents to those they represent, see Alex C. Michalos' "The Loyal Agent's Argument," in T. Beauchamp and N. Bowie, Ethical Theory and Business (Englewood Cliffs, NJ: Prentice Hall, 1979), pp. 338-348.
12. These hardships are well documented in the collections cited above (Nader and Westin).

13. See Parts 4 and 5 for a development of the sense of justice.

14. See Richard de George, "Whistleblowing: Permitted, Prohibited, Required," in Conflicting Loyalties in the Workplace ed. F.A. Elliston (Notre Dame, IN: University of Notre Dame Press, 1985) and his "Ethical Responsibilities of Engineers in Large Organizations: The Pinto Case" (National Conference on Engineering Ethics, Troy, NY: June 20-22, 1980.

15. See Ernest Barker's Social Contract (New York: Oxford University Press, 1960) for a general discussion of these thinkers. For the particular views of Thomas Hobbes, see his Leviathan, ed. Michael Oakeshott (Oxford: Basil Blackwell, 1958), viz. Sections 13-21.

16. See Thomas Aquinas, Summa Theologica I-II, O 95, cit. 2, in Introduction to Saint Thomas Aquinas, ed. Anton C. Pegis (New York: Modern Library, 1948), p. 649. Aquinas cites Augustine's De Lib Arb I, 5 (PL 32, 1227).

17. This position is Thoreau's who reduces the dilemma of the civil disobedient to a simple choice: if the law is just, obey it; if it is unjust, break it. See David Thoreau Walden and Civil Disobedience ed. Owen Thomas (New York: Norton, 1966), pp. 229-231.

18. See, for example, Jeffrie G. Murphy's 'Marxism and Retribution," Philosophy and Public Affairs 2 (1973): 217-243.

19. The case is documented in Alan Westin's collection (see Note 7): Adrienne Tomkins, pp. 69-74.

20. The full position is set forth in A Theory of Justice (Cambridge, MA: Harvard University Press, 1971).

21. In Rawls' application of these to political dissent see his "The Justification of Civil Disobedience," in Today's Moral Problem, ed. Richard Wasserstrom (New York: Macmillan, 1973), pp. 346-357.

22. This position is advocated persuasively in Christopher D. Stone, Where the Law Ends (New York: Harper and Row, 1975), pp. 80-87.

TEN
ANONYMOUS
WHISTLEBLOWING

The purpose in this chapter is to ask whether whistle-blowers are morally justified in concealing their identities while revealing wrongs committed by others? Are people who blow the whistle under a moral obligation to do so publicly? Are they obliged to make their identity known or may they remain anonymous? The prohibition on anonymity is pervasive and strong. What are the alternative rationales for it, and are they sound?

THE CONCEPT OF ANONYMITY

Before turning to an appraisal of anonymous whistleblowing, we need to distinguish anonymity from three related phenomena--ignorance, secrecy, and privacy. In general someone acts anonymously when his or her identity is not publicly known. For example a bomb threat is anonymous when no one knows who wrote the letter or made the telephone call, when others are ignorant of the agent's identity. Yet clearly to say literally that no one at all knows is mistaken; the writer knows that he or she sent the letter, and therefore at least one person knows. It is thus not a matter of total ignorance.

Is an action done anonymously when no one but the agent knows? This notion comes close to the extreme form of secrecy. The greatest secret concerns information I share with no one else. But secrecy in this sense is too extreme, for

how did I come by this information? If someone told me, at least one other person knows. Paradigmatically, information is secret when shared among few people, with two as the limiting case. But it does not suffice that only these two people know and merely by chance no one else. Such "accidental secrets" are not secrets in the strict sense. To qualify as a secret, there must be a conspiracy of silence. It is the exclusion of others, the denial of access by them to information, that marks a secret.

Yet something more is built into the notion of secrecy that becomes clearer if we consider a related concept-- privacy. Information is private when I justifiably deny the right of others to share it. The facts about my sex life or income tax return are private in that others (ordinarily) cannot demand access to them. The domain of privacy is one in which I claim a right to exclude others, unless they can invoke a higher right to override mine.[1]

In the case of privacy, the burden of proof rests with those who would secure access to what is protected under this rubric. In the case of secrecy, the burden of proof is reversed; those who would withhold information must provide the information. In the case of privacy, the presumption is that others should not intrude. In the case of secrecy, the presumption is that something should not be shared. This presumption may be successfully countered by some "top secret" documents with an appeal to national security. Alternatively, in the case of secret acts of espionage, the presumption may not be met; information that is not shared should be, and is, wrongfully and deliberately kept from others.

Is anonymity more like privacy or secrecy? In the case of anonymous whistleblowing, one needs to note that the information kept from others is of a particular sort--namely about a person's identity. Moreover, the sharing of this information may be limited or extensive. To be anonymous, the public must be precluded from knowledge of the individual's identity, but their exclusion does not entail that no one else knows. Anonymity per se is neutral, lying in the middle ground between secrecy and privacy; it entails that the public does not know or have access to the identity of an individual, but it does not locate the burden of proof in withholding this information.

THE RIGHT TO REMAIN ANONYMOUS

Does the public have a right to know the whistleblower's identity, or does he or she have a right to withhold it? Withholding such information strikes many as wrong. But why, and in what sense? Let me suggest several different senses of wrong, which gradually become paradigmatically moral.

A refusal to let one's identity be known could be constructed as bad manners. Blowing the whistle anonymously is like snitching on someone behind his or her back. As kids we were all taught that such tattling was wrong. It is a paradigm of bad manners to say nasty things about people not present to defend themselves. Anonymity in whistleblowers is a breach of manners--faulty etiquette in people who should know better as they act in the more consequential professional world. But why are such breaches of etiquette condemned so harshly, and is this harshness justified?

Typically, the answer is couched in terms of loyalty.[2] To be a faithful member of a group is to protect the interests of that group as a whole and of its members individually. Saying nasty things about people behind their backs disrupts the cohesion of the group, undermining trust in each other and threatening the group solidarity. As a threat to the welfare of the group, individually or collectively, as well as to the very basis of its existence, tattling is severely condemned.

A blanket prohibition on tattling cannot be sustained, as three analogies can serve to demonstrate.

Analogy 1: Suppose my older sister is about to swallow some pills I think may be dangerous. To tell my mother may not be wrong, but right and indeed obligatory. Though I have "blown the whistle" on my sister, if I am doing so for her own good in a situation that is serious and urgent, it is not objectionable--even if I ask mother not to tell on me. Clearly, it is preferable to saying or doing nothing at all. My sister's ignorance may help us to live together, to get along in situations where her anger might be disruptive and counter productive for each of us. Since my sister does not know what I did, I have acted anonymously--at least as far as she is concerned. Even though mother knows, her knowledge, like that of the closed congressional committee to which a whistleblower testifies in camera, does not totally dispel anonymity.

Typically, the childhood scenario is less serious: my sister takes a cookie from the jar without asking, and I squeal on her. My action may be condemned because the incident is trivial. But as the seriousness of the incident increases, the condemnation of anonymous whistleblowing weakens. The extent of the harm threatened is one factor to be weighed in making a moral judgment. The seriousness of the harm the whistleblower seeks to disclose and thereby curtail may be measured in several ways--the number of people affected and the extent to which they are hurt, physically or psychologically. Alternatively, one might appraise this seriousness in less consequentialist terms by invoking deontological principles. Perhaps someone's rights are denied-- such as the right to privacy--even though no physical or psychological harm ensues. Whichever approach one takes, the more serious the offense, the less stringent the prohibition on anonymity.

One might respond that my analogy confuses two different concepts whistleblowing and anonymity. Conceding that the greater the harm threatened, the more one is obliged to blow the whistle, one could nevertheless insist that one should always do so publicly and never anonymously. But consider three possibilities: A blowing the whistle publicly; B blowing the whistle anonymously; and C not blowing the whistle at all. Prima facie, A is morally preferable to B, and B is morally preferable to C. Though this ranking holds at the individual level, one can adopt a rule-utilitarian perspective on the effects of acting anonymously on the practice of whistleblowing; anonymity is justified if it increases the number of people who with good reason blow the whistle, that is, if anonymity promotes the practice of effective, warranted whistleblowing.[3] Accordingly, the first analogy asserts that blowing the whistle anonymously is preferable to not blowing it at all--especially when the particular harm threatened is serious; and it hypothesizes that if a veil of ignorance increases the number of effective and legitimate whistleblowers, the principle of anonymity has a rule-utilitarian defense. But the analogy does not show that anonymously blowing the whistle is always preferable to blowing the whistle publicly. Consider now a second case to elicit a second factor in addition to seriousness.

Analogy 2: The school bully is about to beat up a new kid who looks very frail and helpless. Since I am unable to stop him, I run to the teacher to report the incident. After the teacher has intervened, I ask him not to say I reported the incident. To protect myself from retaliation, I want to remain anonymous. If the bully is very strong and I am very weak, my request is justified; there is no moral reason why I too should suffer unfairly at the bully's hands. By the same token, corporations bully employees who cannot easily defend themselves. Because of their vulnerability, anonymity is warranted. As a second thesis I propose that the greater the probability of unfair retaliation, the weaker the prohibition on anonymity should be.

The literature to date suggests that most whistle-blowers--even those who act for good moral reasons-- pay a very high price for dissenting.[4] In many cases they are fired or demoted, transferred to unattractive assignments or locales, ostracized by their peers, and cast into psychological and professional isolation. Should they try to obtain another job in the same field, they often find they are "blacklisted": many employers do not want to hire someone who "caused trouble" on his or her last job. Moreover, under the prevailing legal doctrine of employment-at-will, fired whistleblowers have only limited legal recourse; in most jurisdictions the courts uphold an employer's right to fire someone for almost any reason.[5] In the absence of such legal protection, the burden of defending himself or herself falls very heavily on the shoulders of the whistleblower alone.

In asserting that the probability of unfair retaliation decreases the strength of the prohibition on anonymity, I do want to distinguish two concepts permissible and obligatory. My point, to put it briefly, is that moral heroism is not and should not be mandated. Though we praise the courage of a professional engineer who speaks out regarding dangerous practices when he or she risks a job, to require extraordinary self-sacrifices demands too much. His or her unwillingness to risk career, personal livelihood, and the means whereby he or she supports the family are perfectly understandable reasons for remaining silent. Indeed, they may justify silence. When such individual self-sacrifice is the only way to protect the public, one must look instead to the development of other mechanisms--the law, the courts, unions, the press, professional associations, or watchdog agencies.

To return to the earlier threefold distinction, blowing the whistle publicly may be ideal, but one cannot demand it. One cannot condemn the persons who act anonymously to protect themselves, those who depend on them, love them, and care for them. There is a limit to what we can ask a person to give up in order to do the right thing. Insofar as anonymity reduces what may be an unfair burden, it reduces an evil while promoting a good.

So far I have identified two factors that enter into an appraisal of anonymous whistleblowing the seriousness of the harm threatened, and the probability of unfair retaliation. Consider now a third factor the social relationship or roles.

Analogy 3: Suppose the bully in the second analogy is my friend. This social bond places an obligation on me to go to him. Even if I am frail and helpless, given that he is my friend, I am duty bound to ask him to stop. Even if he is not my friend but is only a member of my gang, I should not blow the whistle straight away but go to our leader first-- ask him or her to intervene. If that is not possible or fails, recourse to an outside group may be warranted. My third thesis is that the strength of the prohibition on anonymity is a function of the social relationship. The closer the whistleblower stands to the accused, the stronger the prohibition on anonymity.[6] Most whistleblowers feel an "I vs. them" or "us vs. them." Within polarized groups whistleblowers discuss problems with other members of their group, but hesitate--legitimately, I contend--to go outside it without the protection anonymity brings.

This third factor is related to the second; social distance affects the probability of retaliation. If an intermediary can ensure that justice is done within the group, anonymity is less warranted--perhaps unwarranted. If the Federal Office of Professional Responsibility can guarantee that whistleblowers protesting unfair, illegal, or corrupt practices will not suffer for their efforts to correct them, anonymity is less warranted. It is also less needed. But until employees' rights are secure, a veil of ignorance is one of their few safeguards.

So far I have appraised anonymous whistleblowing as wrong in the sense that picking one's nose at an executive board meeting is wrong--a breach of professional etiquette with socially offensive behavior. The primary consideration is then group solidarity and effectiveness. But one could appeal to other considerations.

Anonymity may be condemned because it impedes the pursuit of truth. The person who levels accusations against another while withholding his or her own identity makes it difficult to determine whether what he charges is true or false; we cannot question this person, ask for his or her sources of information, verify his or her accusations--or so it may be argued.

But to assert that we cannot verify anonymous charges at all is too strong and unfounded. Verification, if it is to count as a proof, must be public and repeatable.[7] Consequently, the means whereby the whistleblower verified to himself or herself that what he or she suspected was true must be available to others...if indeed he or she knows the truth. Those who would learn the truth can discover it by the same means the whistleblower used--even though they do not know the whistleblower's identity.

In the movie and book All the President's Men, the character called "Deep Throat" played this role. Without revealing his own identity, he led the two reporters Bernstein and Woodward along a path that provided the evidence they needed to implicate the President in the Watergate break-ins. He did not need to reveal his own identity. It was enough that from the darkness, he provided clues that would trace out a path, perhaps the one he followed but perhaps not, to the truth.

This example suggests a fourth factor--in addition to the seriousness of the offense, the probability of unfair retaliation, and protecting others who stand in social relationship to the whistleblower--the greater effectiveness of whistleblowing when it is done anonymously. By not revealing his identity, "Deep Throat" may arguably have kept the two Washington Post reporters on the trail longer, extending their searches over a greater period of time and to a greater number of individuals. In the case of particular incidents, anonymity may be a spur to greater efforts and to greater effectiveness. If the goal is the correction of injustices, then anonymity has a utilitarian defense as an effective means of promoting this end.

I have also suggested that it may have a rule-utilitarian justification. By providing for anonymous whistleblowing through hot lines on which individuals can report wrongs without revealing their identities, the total number of incidents reported, investigated and corrected may increase. Significantly, fear of retaliation is not the primary reason for individuals not reporting wrongs in government agencies. Their belief that nothing will be done to redeem these wrongs is the single most important factor. But fear of personal consequences is the second most important factor. Anonymity can allay this fear and hence promote more numerous, effective whistleblowings.

Admittedly, in some cases it may be difficult if not impossible for the whistleblower to provide any conclusive evidence that will not reveal his own identity. In such cases, the choice is not between blowing the whistle anonymously and blowing it publicly; rather, the choice is between blowing it publicly and not blowing it at all. Accordingly, I do not assert that anonymity is always possible. But I do assert that where it is possible, we cannot always fault it as a breach of professional etiquette or because it conceals the truth. Consequently, a blanket of condemnation on anonymity is not warranted. Rather, its justification depends on four factors: the seriousness of the offense, the probability of unfair retaliation, the social relationships, and its effectiveness. Let me turn thirdly to practical considerations.

Perhaps anonymity is not a breach of professional etiquette or an obstacle to the truth, but an act of foolishness. The individual who tries to shield himself or herself may find anonymity makes his or her action self-defeating; to be effective one must act publicly--or so one argument may run. What can be said for or against it?

THE EFFICACY OF ANONYMITY

First, one must concede a paradox. The whistleblower attempts to draw public attention to an action he or she regards as wrong, yet is not willing to make his or her own identity public. The means and ends conflict; he or she uses ignorance to promote knowledge, identifies others while hiding. What the whistleblower is trying to do is refuted by the way he or she does it. This paradoxical juxtaposition of means and ends raise our suspicions. It reminds us of those who make war to end war, who deceive to get at the truth, who use force to protect freedom.

Though our suspicions are justifiably aroused, they may turn out to be unjustified. Society may need an institution such as police, based on the legal use of physical force, to protect the freedom of its members. It may indeed be necessary to reveal less than the whole truth to determine if others are telling the truth. We are right to be suspicious when the means contradict the ends, but may find the contradiction only apparent. The whistleblower may succeed at uncovering abusive practices without blowing his or her cover.

Alternatively, our suspicions may be aroused not by the logical paradox but by the question of motives: Why does the whistleblower conceal his or her identity--what does the whistleblower have to hide? To show his or her intentions are pure, we demand the whistleblower stand up and be counted, accept responsibility for his or her actions, and not hide from public view. Hiding makes us think that the whistleblower seeks some private gain rather than the public good, that he or she may be implicated and seeking protection by pointing at others.

A sharp distinction can be drawn between reasons and causes,[8] the justification and the motivation, the evidence that proves a statement true or false, and the personal considerations that lead a person to utter it. Anonymity calls the latter into question, but need not affect the former. Whether the charges are true or false does not depend on the motivation of the individual who levels them. One can appraise the truth of accusations knowing nothing of motives. Whether the whistleblower draws attention to corruption out of spite or altruism makes no difference in one respect; if corruption exists, it should be ended.

Naturally, our attitude toward the whistleblower depends very much on his or her motives. If the whistleblower genuinely seeks the public good, he should be held in high esteem. If the whistleblower does not benefit in any way, his or her altruism is commendable. In appraising the whistleblower's character, his or her motives are of the utmost importance. But in appraising the whistleblower's charges, his or her motives are logically irrelevant.

Two different kinds of moral appraisal are possible--the first focused on the agent and the second focused on the act.[9] In the case of the second, the intention, goal or objective is important for defining the act. We must ask the question: What is it that this action seeks to accomplish? The primary intention in whistleblowing is the disclosure of wrongdoing to the public. Such a disclosure may be motivated by greed, revenge, or simply the desire to retain one's job. Such motives are relevant to the moral appraisal of the agent. In fact many whistleblowers have mixed motives, acting both from a sense of self-interest and a sense of injustice. Whatever their motives, however, for blowing the whistle or remaining anonymous, their action and the practice require independent moral appraisal.

Anonymity can help guard against a fallacious counterattack--an argumentum ad hominem.[10] Individuals called to account by the whistleblower may try to protect themselves by diverting attention to the whistleblower, by shifting the issue from what he or she says to why he or she says it. They may seek to redirect attention from the truth of the whistleblower's claims to the truthfulness of the claimant. But logicians have long recognized this strategy as fallacious. Whether or not what someone says is true does not depend upon his or her personal motive for saying it.

Anonymity may be treated as self-defeating because it calls into question the motives of the whistleblower, but I contend it is wrong to insist it must. However, one genuine issue is raised by this attack on anonymity: How do we distinguish the accusation that should be investigated from those that need not be? A filtering process is needed to make this determination. Anonymity, I contend, is not and should not be the main factor in the filter; one should not decide to investigate a charge only if the person who makes it identifies himself publicly. One is less inclined to investigate anonymous charges because of difficulties anonymity creates--the problems of gathering data, identifying the relevant participants, fixing the time, location, and extent of the act or practice. But then it should be for these reasons, and not because of anonymity per se, that no further action is taken.

From what I have said already, several factors emerge in the determination of the point at which the whistleblower's charges should be investigated. The main factor is the seriousness of the harm to others if the charges are true. Clearly, if the risk to their lives and health is very great, steps must be taken to protect them. The first step is to determine whether the risk is real or imaginary--and

this requires investigating the whistleblower's accusations.
If the whistleblower claims that money has been misspent,
stolen, or siphoned off for illegal purposes, then the greater the amount involved, the more serious the charge and the
greater the need to verify it.

In judging the harm to be done, one must also weigh the
costs of determining this harm. If an investigation is likely to destroy the morale of an otherwise socially useful and
productive organization, an investigation is probably not
warranted. If it is likely to cost more money than might be
saved, then it .is likewise unwarranted. It is the net harm,
after the costs of an investigation have been subtracted,
that must be given moral weight in fixing the threshold.

Should the likelihood that the charges are true be
considered? The objection to giving this probability estimate any weight is that the whistleblower's dilemma arises
precisely because people do not know. An estimate based on
ignorance is unreliable and acting on it irrational. But at
the other extreme, to investigate charges that are preposter-
ous, about events logically impossible or astronomically
remote, will be wasteful if not harmful. Accordingly, the
probability that the charges will prove unfounded should
serve as a factor only to eliminate extreme cases of the pre-
posterous, impossible, or improbable.

So far I have offered three interpretations of the
thesis that whistleblowers should not remain anonymous. On
the first, anonymity is in bad taste--it offends our sense
of etiquette in saying nasty things about someone behind his
or her back. On the second, it is a barrier to the truth.
And on the third, it is in practice self-defeating. I shall
now consider several objections that are more clearly moral
ones.

THE OBLIGATION OF SELF-DISCLOSURE

Several arguments could be developed to explain why
whistleblowers have a moral obligation to disclose their
identity. The two most important appeal to our sense of fair
play and a worry about a slippery slope.

Fair Play

It may be argued that everyone has a right to confront
their accusers. If someone claims I have done something
wrong, I should be allowed to question my accuser face to
face. It violated our sense of fairness to have accusations
leveled against someone who had no opportunity to defend

himself or herself. Does this sense of fair play preclude anonymity among whistleblowers?

In fact we do not always regard concealing one's identity as morally bad. Quite the contrary, we sometimes regard it as good and proper. For example within academia blind reviewing is a wide-spread practice. Members of an editorial board passing judgment on an article submitted for publication may find the author's name removed. Conversely, the reviewers of manuscripts for publication may not reveal their names. In the first case the practice is justified on the grounds that it equalizes the competition. Established authors can less readily exploit their reputations, and the decision to accept or reject an article is made on the basis of quality alone. The second practice supposedly allows more candor; reviewers can offer honest evaluation without fear of reprisals or fear of alienating a colleague with whom they may need to cooperate in the future. Note that in the first case anonymity serves as an equalizer to factor out extraneous and unwarranted influences such as reputation, and in the second case it produces harmony. Insofar as it promotes fairness, equality, or harmony, the practice of concealing one's identity has a moral justification.

In academia we support, for good reasons, a practice analogous to anonymous whistleblowing. Some scholars level criticisms at others without revealing their own identities, and the individuals criticized are denied an opportunity to confront their critics face to face. We support this practice of blind reviewing because it promotes important academic ends--equality of opportunity in publishing and the preeminence of a principle of merit. Those who have their papers rejected in this way cannot claim they have been treated unfairly because they were never allowed to confront their reviewers. At most they have a right to know what the criticisms are and to respond to them. Likewise, we should support anonymous whistleblowing: it provides for an important social end--the redressing of wrongdoing.

By analogy the Office of Professional Responsibility and the inspectors general function as an editorial board. They review criticisms from whistleblowers, sift the evidence and make a determination. Individuals have a right to a fair hearing, but no right to confront their accusers.

I reject the objection to anonymity based on fair play on the grounds that anonymity promotes important social values and that the rights of the accused can be protected in other ways. Anonymity allows individuals to come forward who would otherwise remain silent for fear of reprisals. In so doing it promoted the public welfare, which may be sub-

verted by abuses of power by government officials or the public safety, which may be threatened by dangerous practices
of private industry. It may also promote honesty and accountability among managers who know they will find it difficult
to conceal their indulgences. Admittedly, individuals have a
right to protect themselves against false accusations that
can ruin their careers and compromise their good name. But
to guarantee this right, the identity of whistleblowers need
not be known; it is only necessary that accusations be properly investigated, proven true or false, and the results
widely disseminated.

If the whistleblower and the accused confronted each
other as equals, anonymity would be unnecessary. But typically the power differentials are enormous, and most whistleblowers pay dearly for the action. They lose their jobs, get
transferred to a less attractive, if not unattractive,
locale and assignment, find their family life disrupted, and
their friends and colleagues less amiable. The taunt of the
accused that the whistleblower come forward and "face him
like a man" is a bully's challenge when issued by the powerful. In a court where the judge, lawyers, and legal process
serve as an equalizer, anonymity is less warranted. The prohibition on anonymity denies employees one of their few safeguards from retaliation of powerful aroused enemies. Until
positive steps have been taken to protect employees' rights
to dissent, the condemnation of anonymity discourages one of
the few checks on the abuse of power by corporate or government officials.

The Slippery Slope

Behind the prohibition on anonymity lurks the fear:
What if everyone does that? The need to come forward and be
identified acts as a check on a practice that threatens the
day-to-day operation of bureaucracies, corporations, and
institutions. People have jobs to do, and precious time is
wasted on unproductive activities if they go about secretly
complaining of others--or so the argument may run. Furthermore, to continue this attack, damage is done to the moral
fabric of an organization by anonymous whistleblowers who
destroy the peace and harmony on which a smooth operation is
based. To keep this practice within reasonable bounds and
limit its corrosive impact, we must insist that whistleblowers publicly identify themselves. Without this restriction we slide down a slippery slope into corporate chaos and
institutional anarchy.

What can be said against this slippery argument? First,
it is important to maintain a realistic perspective: How
many more employees would be likely to blow the whistle if

anonymity protected them? The simple answer is: We do not know. Clearly, to argue rationally against a practice, our argument should be based on information--not misinformation, suspicions, and fears. Logically, the slippery slope contention is an **argumentum ad ignoratiam**, a fallacious inference from our ignorance.

Second, it is important to locate clearly the burden of proof: Does it lie with the defenders of anonymity or its critics? As a form of dissent, whistleblowing is an exercise of a highly valued right--freedom of speech. Admittedly, the context is not political but bureaucratic, not dissent against one's government but against one's employer (though for some whistleblowers the two are the same). Insofar as whistleblowers are speaking out, the burden of proof rests with those who would restrict them from exercising their freedom of speech. Until they can demonstrate a clear and present danger to society, and not just to themselves, their fears or hysteria will not serve as adequate moral bases for restricting the rights of others to dissent.

Third, it is important to be clear that this burden will be difficult to sustain, for the right to dissent is not easily overridden. For example though an organization might be destroyed by the actions of an anonymous whistleblower, proving this would not necessarily establish the moral right of the institution's executives to silence the whistleblower. For suppose the institution is a chemical company, polluting the water the public drinks with toxic substances. Given that they have no moral right to endanger the health of others to begin with, they have no right to silence a whistleblower from disclosing this danger--even if the whistleblower's actions threaten their corporate existence.

To establish a right of corporations to silence whistleblowers, one would have to show that society would be better off if corporations had such a right. The very claim that they do or should is dangerously close to the theoretical flourish: What's good for General Motors is good for the country. Today we recognize the dangers of air pollution from automobiles, and the harm of gas-guzzlers to the nation's economy. Such claims can now more readily be seen for what they are—self-deluded or hypocritical attempts to equate corporate profits with the social good. For a utilitarian the burden of proof can be sustained only by demonstrating that restricting the whistleblower's right of dissent will work to the long-term advantage of society, rather than the corporation. I, for one, do not think that the empirical evidence can be marshalled to establish this claim.

CONCLUDING REFLECTIONS

Throughout this chapter I have adopted an approach that could be loosely termed "utilitarian." In so doing I have made myself vulnerable to standard objections to utilitarianism that to some might undermine my analysis completely. Accordingly, I shall conclude with some reflections on my approach. I shall not attempt a defense of utilitarianism per se but only a clarification of the principles on which I have relied and hence the limits of my analysis.

Stated in negative terms, I have not sought to show that anonymous whistleblowing is always justified. Clearly reckless accusations with little or no evidence to substantiate charges can damage an individual's reputation unfairly. I have assumed that those who reveal the wrongs of others have sufficient evidence to persuade a rational person that some wrongdoing has occurred. Otherwise, an individual is not blowing the whistle but just complaining. Given that this epistemic condition is satisfied, I have argued primarily that a blanket prohibition on anonymous whistleblowing is unwarranted.

But to assert that it is not always wrong fails to establish when it is right. To delineate these conditions, I have appealed to four factors the seriousness of wrongdoing, the probability of unfair retaliation, the social relationships, and the effectiveness in redressing wrongs. These four factors function as boundaries to mark the space within which anonymous whistleblowing is defensible.

Within this sphere I contended that three common counter-arguments would not suffice. In more positive terms I argued that anonymous whistleblowing is an effective means to important social ends--the redressing of wrongdoing, the elimination of waste, corruption, illegality, and the abuse of power. My argument is, broadly speaking, "utilitarian" in that it relies on this means-end schema.

One could argue that whistleblowing--whether it be anonymous or not--is morally justified regardless of the social purpose it serves.[11] For example if all employees have the right to freedom of speech, then (anonymous) whistleblowing is simply the exercise of this right and morally justified as such. I have not attempted such a deontological justification here,[12] though I find it a plausible alternative.

I would stress, however, two qualifications on the sense in which my defense is utilitarian. First, the end to which whistleblowing is a means is not the greatest happiness for the greatest numbers. I include justice and the redressing of injustices—whether these will make more people happy or not. And second, I recognize that the pursuit of these ends must be curtailed by respect for rights. These function as side constraints, following Nozick,[13] and impose limitation on what whistleblowers can and cannot do. Due process provisions must be included—not just to protect whistleblowers but those whom they accuse. To delineate more precisely the conditions under which whistleblowing generally, and anonymous whistleblowing in particular, is morally justified, much more needs to be said on these side constraints and due process provisions.

My sympathies have been with whistleblowers, for they in fact frequently suffer the fate of the powerless—their rights are trampled upon, even when their cause is just. Alternatively, one can sympathize with those unfairly accused by whistleblowers, and I recognize the dangers of increasing their numbers by offering whistleblowers a shield of anonymity to hide behind. But from my own research it is clear that the numbers of those unfairly treated are much greater among the ranks of whistleblowers than those they accuse. If one is concerned with the greater injustices, then anonymous whistleblowing is morally defensible.

NOTES

This chapter is a revised version of a paper originally published by F.A. Elliston in The Journal of Business and Professional Ethics (Winter 1982): pp. 39-59.

1. St. Augustine confuses this distinction between privacy and secrecy in his analysis of sexual intercourse, with the results that he regards all sex as evil. See St. Augustine's "Sexual Lust and Original Sin" in The City of God, trans. Philip Levine (Cambridge, MA: Harvard University Press, 1966), pp. 345-401. For a contemporary discussion of privacy as it bears on interpersonal relationships, see Jeffery H. Reiman's incisive "Privacy, Intimacy and Personhood," Philosophy and Public Affairs 6 (1976): 26-44, and the articles he cites by Judith Javis Thompson, Thomas Scanlon, and James Rachels.

2. See Robert M. Anderson et al. Divided Loyalties, (West Lafayette, In.: Purdue University Press, 1980). For an extensive philosophical discussion of loyalty, see Josiah Royce's The Philosophy of Loyalty (New York: Macmillan, 1980).

3. The experience of France, where civil servants are encouraged to report abuses on the government by calling an investigation office, has proven an effective curb on abusive actions and practice. A similar hotline exists in the United States federal bureaucracy.

4. One has only to look to those cases cited by Nader and Westin as well as those that typically make the newspaper headlines.

5. For an excellent discussion of this doctrine, see J.P. Christiansen, "A Remedy for the Discharge of Professional Employees Who Refuse to Perform Unethical or Illegal Acts: A Proposal in Ail of Professional Ethics," Vanderbilt Law Review 28 (1975): 805–841.

6. Very little has been written on stratified moral obligations (and rights) that vary according to one's social relationship or role, though the issue is omnipresent in the fields of professional and applied ethics. For four notable exceptions, see R.S. Downie, Roles and Values (London: Methuen & Co., 1971); Stuart Hampshire (ed.), Public & Private Morality (New York: Cambridge, 1978); Charles Fried, "Rights & Roles" in Right and Wrong (Cambridge, MA: Harvard University Press, 1972), pp. 167-195; and Alan Goldman, The Moral Foundations of Professional Ethics (Totowa, NJ: Littlefield Adams, 1980).

7. For a more detailed analysis of the philosophical issues involved in confirmation, see Carl G. Hempel, Philosophy of Natural Science (Englewood Cliffs, NJ: Prentice Hall, 1966), Chapter 4.

8. For a discussion of these and related concepts see Richard Taylor, Action & Purpose (Englewood Cliffs, NJ: Prentice Hall, 1966), Chapter 10.

9. John Stuart Mill recognizes this distinction between judgments about actions and judgments about agents. See Chapter 2 of his Utilitarianism, ed. Samuel Gorovitz (New York: Bobbs-Merrill, 1971), p. 25.

10. See Irving Copi, Introduction to Logic, 3rd ed., (New York: Collier Macmillan, 1968), p. 61.

11. Robert Ladenson takes this approach in his article "Freedom of Expression in the Corporate Workplace" in Business and Professional Ethics, edited by Michael Pritchard and Wade L. Robinson (New York: Humana Press, 1984), reprinted in F.A. Elliston, ed., Conflicting Loyalties in the Workplace (Notre Dame: University of Notre Dame Press, 1985)..

12. If the parallel between professional dissent and civil disobedience holds, then appeals to deontological principles to justify the latter will also serve to justify the former. For an exploration of some of these, see

"Civil Disobedience and Professional Dissent: A Comparative Appraisal," The Journal of Business Ethics (Spring 1982): 23-28 and Chapter Nine (this volume).

13. See Robert Nozick, Anarchy, State and Utopia (New York: Basic Books, 1974).

APPENDIX I
WHISTLEBLOWING
HYPOTHESES

I. INDIVIDUAL FACTORS

PERSONAL CHARACTERISTICS/TRAITS

Hypothesis 1:   Whistleblowers are relatively strong-minded and strong-willed individuals with relatively high ideals and moral principles that move them to go outside their organization to protect the public from unwarranted or questionable practices.

Hypothesis 2:   Whistleblowing is more likely to occur by individuals who are (a) committed to the formal goals of their organization or to the successful completion of their project; (b) identify with the organization; and (c) have a strong sense of professional responsibility.

PROCESS INTERACTION

Hypothesis 3:   The first stage in the process of whistleblowing begins when an individual or a small group: (a) independently observe illegal, inefficient or unethical practices within their organ-

163

ization; (b) perceive at least tacit support for the validity of their technical analysis of the problem; and (c) perceive the organization to be unresponsive to their concerns.

LABELING

Hypothesis 4: After going public, whistleblowers are "labeled" or stigmatized by their organization and possibly experience reduction in organizational status and power if they are not fired.

II. ORGANIZATIONAL FACTORS

ROLE

Hypothesis 5: Whistleblowing is often a response by a professional who has knowledge about a potentially dangerous problem he sees as being neglected by management, yet who feels powerless to influence the formal decision-making processes in the organization.

Hypothesis 6: Whistleblowing is more likely to occur in organizational roles that are general and diffuse, and allow for more autonomy or managerial discretion, than in roles that are specialized, fragmented, and limited to technical responsibility.

Hypothesis 7: Professionals are more likely to blow the whistle on a nonprofessional or those who belong to another profession due to their sense of professional identification and loyalty.

Hypothesis 8: Blowing the whistle on members of one's own profession will be easier if they were not friends but rather strangers with whom one has little or no personal ties.

Hypothesis 9: Blowing the whistle on role players with whom one does not directly associate on the job will be easier than blowing the whistle on role players one works with on an intimate daily basis.

Hypothesis 10: Whistleblowing is more likely when a role incumbent cannot find a compromising position which is satisfying to conflicting role expectations.

Hypothesis 11: Whistleblowing is more likely to occur when there is intrarole consensus (agreement on appropriate role behavior among the role incumbents) and interrole dissension (disagreement between incumbents and nonincumbents on appropriate role behavior).

Hypothesis 12: Whistleblowing is more likely to occur when the individual can remain "anonymous" and does not need to go public by "name."

SYSTEMS/CONTROL

Hypothesis 13: Whistleblowing is more likely to occur in organizations that are closer to System-I (exploitative/autocratic controls) than System-4 (participative-democratic controls).

Hypothesis 14: Whistleblowing is more likely to occur in organizations characterized by hierarchical and centralized control systems.

CULTURE

Hypothesis 15: Whistleblowing is more likely to occur in organizations whose culture emphasizes such values as economic efficiency, accountability, growth, and strict loyalty, while down-playing attention to questionable practices and unethical behavior on the part of individuals in the organization.

Hypothesis 16: If top management does not value and reward the reporting of unethical and questionable practices, whistleblowing is more likely to occur.

WORK GROUP

Hypothesis 17:   Whistleblowing is more likely to occur when the work group offers both technical and emotional support.

SIZE

Hypothesis 18:   Whistleblowing is more likely to occur in large-scale and complex organizations.

TECHNOLOGY

Hypothesis 19:   Whistleblowing is more likely to occur in organizations with more technologically complex tasks.

CHANGE

Hypothesis 20:   Whistleblowing is a form of organizational guidance that attempts to span organizational boundaries and affect the relationship between one organization and another.

Hypothesis 21:   Whistleblowing is more likely to occur in organizations that do not provide for dissent inside or outside its formal control system.

III. ENVIRONMENTAL FACTORS

THE ORGANIZATION AND ITS ENVIRONMENT

Hypothesis 22:   Whistleblowers occupy "unofficial" boundary positions in the organization and point out matters of concern for the welfare of the organization's relationship to the environment.

FORCES IN THE ENVIRONMENT

Hypothesis 23: Whistleblowing is more likely to occur with the rise of new scientific and complex technologies and developments.

Hypothesis 24: Whistleblowing is more likely to occur when the economy is in a deteriorating cycle than in times of economic prosperity or growth.

Hypothesis 25: Whistleblowing is more likely to occur when government regulatory activity increases.

Hypothesis 26: Whistleblowing is more likely to occur when greater accountability is demanded by the public of government officials.

Hypothesis 27: Whistleblowing is more likely to occur when higher standards are expected of professionals or employees in private industry.

Hypothesis 28: Whistleblowing is more likely to occur when there is increasing public concern for environmental, health, and safety problems.

Hypothesis 29: Whistleblowing is more likely to occur when the media attaches more importance to "white collar" deviance.

TYPES OF ENVIRONMENT

Hypothesis 30: Whistleblowing is more likely to occur when organizations do not effectively adapt to changes in their "turbulent" environments.

Hypothesis 31: Whistleblowing is more likely to occur when organizations rigidly conform to past practices rather than adopt new practices more suitable to their changed environments.

APPENDIX II
THE WORD PROCESSOR

In this project on the uses and abuses of science and technology, three pieces of equipment were important to us: the telephone, which was used to interview subjects; the tape recorder, which was used to maintain a record of the interviews; and a word processor. Though the original budget did not include a line item for word processing equipment, we recognized an urgent need as we attempted to transcribe the interviews. Once it was acquired, it proved tremendously useful.

THE INTERVIEWS

Transcribing the Interviews

In order to make full use of the interviews, it was decided that a written transcript would be made. These transcripts would make the interviews much more accessible to all the members of the project, and they would enhance their usefulness to each member of the staff.

However, the problems involved in transcribing them seemed almost unending. In order to keep the costs down, early interviews were sent to outside typists who could work on them at home, either during the evenings or on weekends. If the typists were paid on an hourly basis, their work was very conscientious--but the corresponding costs high. And if they were paid on a per page basis, the costs were lower but the transcripts frequently full of errors.

Proper names were difficult to decipher, and some passages were barely audible. Consequently, despite the best efforts of fine typists, the results were uneven. The first draft of a transcript was inevitably full of inaccuracies, and not at all the kind of work we would be proud to submit for approval to a senior executive whom we had interviewed. It was invariably necessary to retype major portions of the transcript, if not the entire transcript, in order to produce a readable and presentable version. The typing costs doubled, and threatened to triple.

Moreover there were editorial problems that we had not anticipated. The typists, none of whom were familiar with the project, were instructed to be accurate above all else. The result was a literal transcript that reproduced on the printed page all the speakers' pauses, repetitions, and false starts. These were tiresome and distracting to read. If we wanted a more readable transcript, another typing would be required. The prospect of expending an enormous proportion of the budget in order to obtain an accurate and readable transcript led us to look at word processing equipment.

The advantage of a word processor is that it allows considerable changes to be made without the necessity of retyping the unchanged portions. By first transcribing the interview onto a word processor, we could reduce the typing costs to one typing. The interviewer could then review the transcript while listening to the tape recording and make the corrections--either on a hard copy run off from the word processor, or on the machine directly. The costs of the rental could be recouped by the saving in typing and reentering time.

Editing and Fictionalizing the Transcripts

Once the decision was made to obtain a word processor for transcribing the interviews, other uses of the machine were discovered. In the early phases of the project, the interviews were to be analyzed and the results tabulated. To do so, it was obviously not necessary to have anything more than an accurate and readable transcript. But shortly after the word processor was acquired, it was decided to incorporate portions of the interviews into the case write-ups. For this purpose we needed a transcript that was not just accurate and readable, but grammatical, clear, and (if possible) compelling. Accordingly, the transcripts were edited for style and cleaned up--grammatical errors were corrected and long rambling sentences were divided. The result was a transcript that was more than literate--it was literary.

Later in the project, the word processor was used on the transcripts for another purposes to change all the names. As a result of the Institutional Review Board's concern for confidentiality, we were required to fictionalize all the cases. The global search on the word processor provides for the easy substitution of one name for another. This procedure made it much easier to produce a fictionalized version of the transcript on which all the names had been changed.

The Bibliography

For our preliminary work on this project, we undertook an extensive survey of newspapers and magazines in order to identify a large number of whistleblowing cases from which we could select our own cases.

In addition to surveying popular materials, we needed to survey the scholarly literature to develop a theoretical framework from which we could approach our cases. The primary theoretical literature surveyed was in organizational theory and professional ethics.

In the course of conducting this literature search, we discovered that Dr. James Bowman of Wyoming University had compiled a bibliography on whistleblowing. It was tempting to approach him about combining our work on popular and current literature with his earlier listing to produce a comprehensive bibliography on professional dissent. We succumbed to the temptation.

A major difficulty with any bibliography is keeping it current. As new literature appears, one's bibliography is constantly threatened with becoming out of date. Accordingly, it was decided to use a word processor. The advantages were threefold: first, the list could be continuously brought up to date; second, any errors could be easily corrected; and third, the publisher could be given a camera-ready copy.

Unfortunately, we decided to enter the information on the word processor at Dr. Bowman's institution. At the time this seemed appropriate. His university has a professional typist; the costs were reasonable; and our own staff was hard pressed with their own work. In retrospect, however, it was a costly but unforeseeable mistake. Dr. Bowman changed institutions shortly after the first complete draft was entered, and his new university--while it could provide him with free word processing facilities--had incompatible equipment. To accommodate revisions the entire bibliography had to be reentered. Moreover, since his university is now introducing new equipment, we are faced with the prospect of a third typing.

None of this would have been necessary if the bibliography had first been entered on our own equipment--or if the manufacturers made compatible machines. But at present the word processors of each manufacturer, and indeed each model, cannot interface with other equipment.

Drafting Materials

In writing up the cases, the word processor has proven to be very useful to all the staff. It has a number of features that have enabled us to make extraordinarily good use of our writing time. A word processor can perform several operations on a text that facilitates composition.

1. Corrections. It is very easy to correct a mistake--just type over it. The correction is immediately made on the screen and on any hard copies that are run.
2. Spelling Mistakes. The word processor obtained has a dictionary with 100,000 words in it and the capacity to add 2,000 more. Whenever a text is entered, a spelling check will determine if any word typed is not in the dictionary. Proper names can be added or by-passed. The spelling check is not exhaustive: it will not discriminate between "them" and "then" (since both are in the dictionary), but it will quickly identify common typographical errors such as inversions.
3. Shifting Texts. The word processor allows you to block out a word, sentence, paragraph, or page, shift it into memory, and insert it anywhere you would like. When materials are subject to major reorganization, this feature is very handy.
4. Additions and Deletions. You can open up space anywhere in a text to insert a word, sentence, paragraph or additional pages. Conversely, you can delete any amount of text.
5. Replacements. On a global search, substitutions can be made. This was particularly useful in fictionalization, but could also be used as an economy measure. For example, instead of typing out "word processor" every time this phrase is used, one can type WP and substitute on a global search.
6. Assembling Documents. Sometimes it is preferable to type documents in portions--for example when different people are responsible for different parts of a case--and then to assemble all

the sections into one chapter. The assemble feature allows this to be done easily.

7. <u>Merging Documents</u>. For sending out one letter to several people, a form letter can be merged with a list of names and addresses to produce an individualized letter. This procedure avoids typing the same letter more than once. Alternatively, if each base letter needs to be tailored to the recipient, the letter can be entered, copied, and then revised. Again it is unnecessary to retype the standard portions, thereby economizing on time.

8. <u>Reproduction</u>. Once materials have been entered on the word processor, an original can be run with up to four clean carbon copies. The photocopying costs can thereby be reduced substantially, as well as the demands on staff time.

Some Pitfalls

The clear consensus among the staff was that the monies were better spent on a word processor than on secretarial time. If the $270/month was used to purchase 12 hours per week of secretarial time, it would not have been as useful. But this efficiency depends on the willingness and the ability of the staff to use the equipment. Project personnel who were not adept typists would not find this arrangement preferable, nor would those who resist mastering complicated new equipment. But frequently, capable people can write a letter or type a report in less time than it would take to compose the draft and then explain to a secretary exactly what needed to be done.

Yet there are definite costs associated with the use of the word processor beyond the time actually spent on the equipment. First, there are the training costs. To learn the basic operating features of the machine probably takes about ten hours. In this period an experienced typist can learn how to enter materials--how to open and close files, print a hard copy, and make minor corrections. It probably requires an additional ten hours to master some of the basic editing functions--how to move texts, perform global searches, and merge documents. If time is not set aside specifically for learning these procedures, the rate of work will be slowed down during this learning period--representing an additional cost.

One must also reckon the costs of mistakes. While one is learning the equipment, errors will be made--not just typing errors but mistakes that could accidentally delete a paragraph, a page, or an entire document. The time to correct these errors must be entered into the calculation.

It is unavoidable that some human errors be made. But word processors are powerful machines--they can be a tremendous help or a tremendous bother. Losing a 60-page manuscript can be a costly mistake.

Moreover, such a cost can be incurred through no fault of the operator. Word processors are very sensitive to static electricity: walking across a rug can create a charge that will drive the machine crazy. A page or an entire disc can get mangled. By keeping a hard copy of all the materials on the disc, or a back-up of the disc, the costs of accidents can be reduced, but they can never be eliminated.

Some mistakes are innocuous and amusing. In fictionalizing one of our cases, we wanted to substitute the name "Kelly" for "Stone". The machine can be instructed to take heed of upper and lowercases, and to stop at each occurrence. But if one is confident and pressed for time, one can tell the machine to repeat the substitution for all cases without stopping. One unfortunate victim of this procedure was an engineer who became afflicted with a gallkelly.

NOTES

1. For a more philosophical discussion of the uses of word processors, see John Snapper and Frederick Elliston, "Word Processors: Methodological and Moral Issues." Sixth International Conference on Computers and the Humanities, Raleigh: NC: June 6-8, 1983.
2. Eventually it was published as Professional Dissent (New York: Garland, 1983).

INDEX

INDIVIDUALS

Van Schaick, J., 132
Vollmer, H.M., 45

Weil, Vivian, 23, 24
Waters, James, 58, 73
Westin, Alan, 5, 10, 17, 12,
    52, 71, 74, 144
Whyte, William, 90, 95
Winkler, Karen J., 95
Wolfgang, Marvin, 85
Woodward, 150
Wrightsman, Lawrence S., 53

Young, Stanley, 46

ORGANIZATIONS

Bay Area Rapid Transit (BART)
    7, 10, 24, 45, 68, 70
Department of Agriculture
    111
Department of Health, Education
    and Welfare (HEW), 111
Deparatment of Housing and Urban
    Development, 111
Environmental Protection Agency
    (EPA), 9
Federal Drug Administration
    (FDA), 15
Federal Bureau of Investigation
    (FBI), 11, 23, 109
Federal Labor Relations Authority
    (FLRA), 106
Fund for Constitutional Government
    103
General Accounting Office
    (GAO), 109
Hindelang, Michael J.,
    Research Center, v, 63
Institute for Policy Studies (IPS)
    52
Merit System Protection Board
    (MSPB), 100, 106–108, 113
Navy Fuel Supply Office
    (NFSO), 5, 9

National Opinion Research Center
    (NORC), 70
Office of Special Counsel (OSC)
    100, 107–109, 113
United States Congress, 9, 20, 51,
    103–105, 107, 109–111, 117, 119,
    121–122, 124, 128, 129–130,
    138, 139
United States Senate
    15, 23, 11, 117

ACTS

Atomic Energy Act, 105
Civil Service Reform Act, 100
Federal Mine Safety and Health Act
    105, 116
Federal Water Polution Control Act
    105
First Amendment, 76, 100, 102–103, 112
Inspector General Act, 100
Longshoremans and Harbor Workers Act
    105
Michigan Whistleblowers Bill, 105
Nuremburg Code, 138
Occupational Safety and Health Act
    (OSHA), 105
Resource Conservation and Recovery Act
    105
Surface Mining Reclamation Act, 105
Toxic Substance Control Act, 105

NEWSPAPERS

Congressional Record, 11,
Federal Times, 50, 116, 117
Free Press, 6
Los Angeles Daily Journal, 23
Los Angeles Herald Examiner, 6
New York Times, 23, 54, 115
Wall Street Journal, 23
Washington Post, 23
Washington Star, 116

PLACES

COURT CASES

ABOUT THE AUTHORS

FREDERICK A. ELLISTON, Associate Professor of Philosophy at the University of Hawaii, served as Principal Investigator for the project on whistleblowing that produced this volume. He holds a PhD in philosophy from the University of Toronto and has taught at Trinity College, York University and the State University of New York at Albany. In addition to books on Husserl, Heidegger and Sartre he has published collections in crime, feminism and human sexuality. His most recent work deals with criminal justice ethics.

JOHN KEENAN, Dean of Business and Public Service Administration at Beaufort Technical College, was Research Associate on this project. Dr. Keenan taught previously at St. Rose College and Empire State College in New York. He has written on various topics in business, industry and professional life.

PAULA LOCKHART, Assistant to the Executive Director of Adult Learning at the State Department of Education in New York, served as Research Assistant on the whistleblowing project. She holds a Masters degree from the School of Criminal Justice at the State University of New York at Albany. She coauthored with Drs. Elliston and Bowman Professional Dissent: An Annotated Bibliography and Resource Guide.

JANE VAN SCHAICK served as Research Assistant on the whistleblowing project. She graduated from St. Rose College and is completing an MBA at the Illinois Institute of Technology. She is Executive Director of the Chicago Research Institute and Associate at the Institute for Business Ethics at DePaul University. In addition to conducting research on quality of work life (QWL) and economic development, she has published Legal Ethics: An Annotated Bibliography and Resource Guide, with Dr. Elliston.